MW01355943

The Frayed Ends of Sanity

Tellwell Talent
www.tellwell.ca

ISBN
978-0-2288-2089-5 (Hardcover)
978-0-2288-2088-8 (Paperback)
978-0-2288-2090-1 (eBook)

Dedications

To my wife: You are the most beautiful woman in the world. You mean everything to me, and without you I would be absolutely lost. It's because of you that I was blessed with the opportunity to see many things in life through a different lens. You will always be my dream come true.

To my sister and brother-in-law: I will never be able to thank you enough for the endless support you offered me and my family over the years. Without you I'm not sure how this all would've panned out. You have always been my rock, and you always will be.

Foreword

I am not a perfect human being, or a perfect parent for that matter, nor have I ever claimed to be either one of those things. I don't always make the right decisions although I try to do the best I can in all aspects of my life including the items I mentioned above.

Disclaimer

Names throughout this manuscript have been changed to respect the privacy of my wife and children, especially my two eldest boys. Similarly, some of the places may have been moved and dates altered. Nonetheless, this is a true story.

One

I guess this all began back when I was a teenager—the building blocks from that point in my life formed the foundation for everything that happened after. As a man now in my forties, the last thing I want to do is start throwing blame around about the things that were wrong in my life and how they led the way to my demise. But this is where it began.

The truth is, by the time I was sixteen years old, I was so lost in my life that I didn't know which way was up. There was no way, moving forward, I could have ever made a well-informed proper decision for myself. It just wasn't possible. Low self-esteem coupled with lack of direction and no interest from my parents soon led to my ejection from their home followed by me dropping out of school. And in the mix of all this was the one thing that I felt got me through the day-to-day chaos surrounding me, the one thing in my life that seemed to make sense—a relationship that I was too young to navigate and too desperate to let go of.

Her name was Cheryl, and I was very much in over my head.

All that is enough of a clusterfuck to leave anybody questioning the meaning of life, and when my relationship with Cheryl came to its inevitable end, I was ruined. And when *that* happened, I let my guard down, and in those uncertain times of my life, mired in loneliness, desperation, and (most likely) depression, I let the wrong person in.

I met *her* in the spring of 1996 after I moved away from my hometown of Westlock and found myself in Edmonton.

I was nineteen years old and had made the move for a couple of different reasons. First, when Cheryl broke up with me, I needed to try and get on with my life and couldn't do that living in a small town where she also resided. Second, I knew that there was no future for someone like me in a small town, and the fact that I had dropped out of school would only assure that I would never find a good job there. If I had any hope in hell of getting on with my life and finding a job along the way, one that would someday allow me to do some of the things my heart aspired to do, the big city was my best bet.

I had landed a job making deliveries for a small furniture company in Edmonton, and soon thereafter, my friend Scott and I decided to move in together. As fate would have it, Ashley lived in a development located right next door. She was a short, quiet, vanilla brunette a little younger than me, and like me she'd made the poor decision for herself of dropping out of school. Ashley wasn't employed at the time we met, and as her days were devoid of any responsibility or schedules, she would walk by our place frequently going here or there, and eventually we ended up striking a conversation which is what set the ball rolling in all this.

Scott had been in a relationship for a couple years already with his girlfriend at that time, and a few months into our lease, he informed me that when the lease expired he'd decided to move into his girlfriend's place and take things to the next level with her.

As it turned out, Scott and I had moved into a very rough neighbourhood in Edmonton anyway and I wanted to relocate to a completely different part of the city, and so it all worked out in the end. I can't even begin to describe how lost I was during those days of my life and how much I missed Cheryl. In truth, I went on thinking about her for many years after she had ended things between us. Essentially that rebound made me almost desperate in needing someone to be around, and so I made the decision to ask Ashley if she wanted to move in with me at the end of the lease.

It was the fall of 1996. Scott and I had fulfilled our contractual obligations to the landlord, so we loaded up our shit and parted ways. Scott moved not far from where he and I had lived together, while Ashley and I moved to the west end of the city right off of Groat Road. It was a quiet little complex called Baywood Park, and I felt much better living there. Not only was it cheaper, but it was also a much safer place to live—and being from a small town, that was something that was important to me. I made it clear to Ashley prior to us moving in together that maintaining full-time employment was something that was non-negotiable in our relationship, and so she found a job close to where we lived, cooking in a restaurant shortly after we relocated.

In the months preceding this move, I had been presented with the opportunity to be indentured into an apprenticeship program for the plumbing trade, and I wasted no time in taking full advantage of it. It was this opportunity that reinforced for me that the choice to move from the small town life that I knew and into the big city had indeed been the right decision. The future was brighter than it had ever been as far as my career was going, but other area's of my life at that time such as my relationship with Ashley was beginning to show sign's of weakness. The relationship between Ashley and I was always somewhat toxic. That was true right from the get-go, and looking back now, I know that was simply because we had built the relationship on the wrong foundation. From the start, it was nothing more than convenience for either of us, and fabricating that relationship on those terms certainly meant that it wasn't going to stand the test of time. It couldn't.

Over time, our relationship just became comfortable, convenient, and easy, so instead of choosing to part ways in search of more compatible partner, I just left well enough alone. It was the summer of 1999 when the word came down that big changes were on the horizon and that things in my life were never going to be the same again.

Ashley was pregnant, and we made the decision to keep the baby.

I remember the feeling of anxiety I had when I heard the news, and immediately my thoughts went right to what my parents were going to say about it. I mean, I wasn't married and had no intention of getting married based solely on the fact I was having a baby. I wasn't even in a healthy relationship for that matter, and in keeping with the truth, this pregnancy wasn't something that we had planned. It just happened and that was that.

When I did sit my parents down to tell them what was happening, I could tell they were disappointed that my actions had led to this. I will never forget the cold look my mom gave me after I told them. It wasn't that they weren't going to accept their first grandchild—it just wasn't the way they had envisioned it would all unfold.

Those were undoubtably scary and uncertain times in my life, and I knew it was going to be tough. We were still living at Baywood Park and I was concerned because I knew making the transition from renting an apartment to becoming a homeowner was going to be significantly harder now than it ever would have been without these new circumstances in play.

In March of 2000, Ashley gave birth to a little boy we named Josh, and with his arrival the process of being a parent for the first time began for both Ashley and me. Obviously, this was a huge game changer, and no matter how prepared a person may think they are for having their first child, they never truly are. We certainly weren't.

Seeing as Ashley and I were not overly compatible in the first place, it only assured the process would be much harder than I ever could have anticipated. As it turned out, Josh was colicky and cried for hours and hours on end every single night for the first eight months. Needless to say, that added another level of stress to an already strained relationship.

These were terribly trying times and an absolute worst-case scenario first-time parenting experience for anyone having their first baby. However, time passed, life went on, and Ashley and I came out on the other side of a stressful two thirds of a year alive and sane. Having said that, before Josh had turned one, Ashley and I discovered that she was pregnant again, and although I knew that we were better equipped at that point than we had been before, I was still extremely nervous about doing it all again.

November of 2001 marked the arrival of my second son, Edward. And with his arrival came a much different baby and a much different parenting experience than what we had with Josh.

Edward was pretty much a polar opposite of his brother, and the whole process with him was much easier. It was during this time we packed up our stuff and left Edmonton in the rear-view mirror, moving to a small town to the northeast called Gibbons.

Things between Ashley and I had been on the steady decline the last few years, and a mutual unwillingness to deal with the issues between us would ultimately lead to us parting ways in the fall of 2003. At the time Josh was three and Edward was only just coming up to his second birthday.

Ashley took the kids and moved from Gibbons to a small city called Fort Saskatchewan which was located about fifteen minutes away.

Two

So there I was at twenty-six with two small kids, a separation, and the biggest shitshow of all time getting ready to rear its ugly head.

I think it was pretty obvious right from the word go that this wasn't going to be a run-of-the-mill separation. The scenarios were inconceivable and undoubtedly the telltale signs of the nightmare that lay ahead. These were uneasy times for me as I had never dealt with anything like this before, and none of the details were worked out yet.

In hindsight, I don't think any of the details ever really did get worked out.

I had so many things running through my head. I was worried what the day-to-day life of the kids would look like under Ashley's care. I was worried that proper supervision might not be in place at all times. I was worried about the influence of all the new people coming and going would have on the kids. I was worried I'd miss out on things because the kids and I lived apart now. I was worried about stability. The list in my mind went on and on.

The only reassuring thing to me at that time was knowing I wasn't going anywhere. I knew I would always stay involved in my kids' lives no matter what and they would always know who their dad was. Even though I was just a young man with a world of problems gathering on the horizon, I knew what I had to do.

Turns out these problems ended up being much bigger than I could ever have imagined.

In the early stages of the separation, the kids would stay with Ashley during the day and come to my house at night, and we would split the weekends. I knew that this wasn't the best arrangement for the kids, but in my mind, it was a place to start—we could always make changes down the line, and in all honesty, I was just thankful to have the time I did with the kids. There were however, red flags popping up right from the first day Ashley took up residence on her own.

Almost immediately, I took note that each day I would pick the kids up from Ashley's place the two of them smelled strongly of cigarette smoke. That was something that really bothered me, and I was a smoker myself at the time. Ashley and I had always maintained a smoke free home since our children had come into the world because I didn't want them to be held captive in an environment like that but also for a much more crucial reason. Edward had asthma, and cigarette smoke, of course, is a huge trigger for asthmatics. It was something that I kept front and centre in my mind. I had no issue not having a smoke on the way home while my kids were present or waiting until I was somewhere it wouldn't affect them before I lit one up.

These sorts of considerations were of no concern to Ashley whatsoever.

Ashley and her roommates—and anybody visiting—had little to no regard for the asthmatic toddler in the room. I remember picking the kids up one day after work and she was sitting in a chair in her living room, holding Edward *while smoking a cigarette.* That really tells you a lot, doesn't it? I just can't comprehend how little you must care about the well-being of your child to prioritize your smoking habit over their health. To this day, I still shake my head when I think about it.

The company she was keeping around the kids at the time was another issue. She had people moving in and out constantly, with little to no regard for their backgrounds or whether they were even suitable to be around the kids. Some of these people were questionable to say the least. On top of people moving in and out incessantly, she had started to move herself regularly.

I'm not exactly sure why, but I can certainly speculate that it was due to not paying her bills.

She never stayed in one place long, and that trend of moving was only destined to accelerate as time went on. It was also during this time that the endless stream of different guys she was dating had started to flow as well. Between you, me, and the fence post—*damn*, there was a lot of guys. Funny thing with that, too, they all had one thing in common.

According to Ashley, they were all going to be the *new* father for my kids.

Every swinging dick who walked through that door, according to her, was her soulmate and a better father than I could ever be. Apparently, these new guys had full intentions of taking over my role as Josh and Edward's dad. Some were more invested in the idea than others, but none ever did. Well, actually one tried, but he was a fucking idiot anyways, and that whole relationship between him and Ashley crashed, burned and wound up in the shithouse. But I don't want to get ahead of myself.

I'm still not sure what Ashley thought the outcome of all that dating would be or why she thought the outcome could ever be any different, but that certainly didn't stop her from trying and dragging the kids along with her. It was always awkward for me to have to meet these guys, who were basically living with my kids, and have them judge me based on what she was telling them. And then a short while later—lather… rinse… repeat—the process started again with someone new. I don't know how she wasn't completely ashamed and embarrassed of herself after all the stupid things she said, tried, and did. But over the years, I never saw so much as a glimmer of embarrassment from her for anything.

I'm embarrassed for her. Truthfully, I'm embarrassed to be associated with her.

I honestly can't even find a word in the dictionary to describe how I feel about her. She has always left a blemish of unethical behaviour everywhere she's been, one that has tarnished not only her own reputation but the kids' reputations as well—and occasionally mine.

It became clear, early on for me, that we needed to modify the parenting arrangement we had initially made. I was burning the candle at both ends, working all day, watching the kids at night and every second weekend while Ashley, who was primarily unemployed, had all the time in the world to do absolutely nothing. We ended up making a verbal agreement that we would do a fifty–fifty split custody arrangement with Josh and Edward, and we would accomplish this by them spending a week at a time at each household. I was happy about that. It still gave me time with my kids plus some time to myself to recoup. This was a good way to equally spread the workload of the kids out between us.

Sounds simple enough, but even that had to be difficult.

There was no room for variation if it was impinging on her week off from the kids. There could have been a death in my family, and she would've expected me to be on time to pick the kids up. I remember multiple times at work being asked to stay late for different reasons and having to decline because she refused to keep the kids for a couple more hours. It wasn't like I strayed far from our agreement often anyways, but if I needed to *for any reason at all* there was no way she would allow it. If I was late because there was an accident on the way to get the kids and traffic was slow, she would seriously get pissed off about it. She was *that* unrealistic about it, and man, she loved to preach to me.

This, of course, was a one-way street.

If she had something come up and needed me to keep the kids for a couple extra hours or overnight even, she had no problem communicating that to me as well as her expectation that I do it. To this day, she has never had a problem calling in a favour from me, but she has made it quite clear not to ever ask for one in return. It's really odd. As it turned out in the end, the whole fifty–fifty split parenting agreement proved ineffective anyways and was soon to change.

Ashley had started to discover the endless government resources available to single parents with low to no income, and she wasted no time taking advantage of whatever she could. One of these things was subsidized daycare fees. When she made that discovery, she immediately enrolled the kids full-time in daycare even though she didn't even have a job. She was quick to inform me that any of the unsubsidized fees would be my responsibility to square away with the daycare. Take note of that "my responsibility" statement because according to Ashley everything was my responsibility.

It wasn't long thereafter that I was approached by the owner of the daycare one day while picking the kids up after work. She felt compelled to voice her concerns to me about the length of time the kids were in her care during the weeks that Ashley had them. They were literally there from open until close. So while purposely unemployed and laying around home doing absolutely nothing, the kids were spending twelve hours a day at a daycare during her week of care. I had a full-time job with a commute, and I could still have them picked up and home in or around the ten-hour mark. The daycare owner was fully aware that Ashley was unemployed and that only added to her concern over the issue.

I was seriously shocked. I didn't even know what to say.

Those poor kids, that would be a long day for anybody. It was a really sad state of affairs. You just have to wonder what kind of person has no qualms about putting their kids into a daycare and then going home unemployed and pretending their kids don't exist for twelve hours. It's really sad when you think about it.

When I confronted Ashley on the issue, she basically told me it was none of my business.

"It's not your week so don't worry about it."

It was almost as though she felt that somehow made what she was doing appropriate or justified. I would pick the kids up after work on the Monday from daycare, and my week would begin. Then I would drop them off on the way to work the following Monday at the daycare and Ashley's week would start.

Every other Monday—the start of my week with the kids—would begin with me finding them both sleeping on the floor at five o'clock in the afternoon at the daycare. They were exhausted from a week of inconsistent routines. It always took a couple days to get them back into the routine of the mornings at my house. I had a full-time job to maintain, so things had to go like clockwork in the mornings in order for me to get them dropped off at daycare and still get to work on time. Usually by the time I got them back into a routine, it was Ashley's week again. It was during this time that Josh started kindergarten at a school in Fort Saskatchewan, increasing the necessity for him to be on a consistent schedule each day—on the plus side it also offered him a chance to escape the daycare during Ashley's weeks even if just for a few hours.

So in a nutshell, there was a bunch of strange men trying to father Josh and Edward, they were being moved frequently, living with inconsistent schedules, and spending excessive time in a daycare during my off weeks. And yet according to Ashley I was the useless piece of shit in this equation.

As previously mentioned, Ashley was now starting to take note of all the government resources available to her. I fully understand why these types of government programs exist and why they are necessary and important. There are single parents out there who may lack help or support from the other parent or who may have disabilities that prevent them from being able to provide for their families. I assure you Ashley is not one of these people. She is simply lazy. To this day, I'm not sure how someone who just chooses not to have employment can still have all the resources of the government funded by taxpayers like myself at their disposal.

Once Ashely started investigating the angles available to her it wasn't long before I received word in a letter informing me that a mediation session had been set up, by Ashley, to discuss child support for Josh and Edward. I'll be honest in saying that, at the time, I was a bit confused about it all.

We still had a fifty–fifty split custody agreement in place with Josh and Edward, but now I had to pay her on top of that as well?

Ashley was unemployed by choice. She was fully capable of working, she just refused to do so. Nevertheless, according to family law, it was my responsibility to pony up the difference based on what I made. Even in the event that I did have to pay, Ashley could have been working full-time herself and generating income thus better balancing the required contributions from each of us which would only have benefited the kids anyways.

I firmly believe that any parent who prides themselves as a parent would naturally feel the desire to contribute to generating the resources required to bring their children up to the best of their ability. Not Ashley. Instead, she minimized the amount she made in order to maximize what I had to pay. In truth I found the process to be quite frustrating.

When the mediation day arrived, during introductions, I could read it in the mediator's eyes and through her demeanour towards me that she assumed I was a deadbeat. I was already labelled, there was no doubt about that. I'm certainly not implying that this is the case with all mediators dealing with these situations, but in this case it certainly was. It's also entirely possible—probable even—that her years working as a mediator coloured her view of the situation. To her I was a non-contributing parent. According to Ashley, the mediator told her after the session that she suspected I may have been using drugs because I was red in the face and angered throughout the process.

To this day I'm not sure how else a person could possibly be expected to respond being put in that position.

Essentially, I was being told that, even though my ex was willfully unemployed while I was working a full time job including overtime, I needed to work harder and give more. The exact words from that mediator's lips (I kid you not):

"I understand you work hard, sir, but you need to step it up for your kids here."

My monthly child support payment, according to legislated guidelines, was set at four hundred dollars. So if you crunch some numbers here, I was already paying for all expenses related to the kids for the fifty percent of the time they were with me, plus any of the daycare fees that were outstanding each month, and now another four hundred dollars a month on top of that just because Ashley refused to work and wasn't bringing any revenue into the equation. I was made solely responsible, that day, for over eighty percent of all expenses regarding Josh and Edward, and this was something that was legislated and enforced by the government.

On a more positive note, my story, even then, wasn't all doom and gloom.

Three

In October of 2005, in the midst of all the dark difficult times I had been dealing with, a light appeared in the distance, signalling that my life was about to turn around.

I was installing a plumbing system in a hotel in Fort Saskatchewan at the time. Like most of the Canadian population—certainly most of the people in Fort Saskatchewan—Tim Horton's was my daily coffee stop of choice. One day while sitting down having a coffee with an elderly gentleman I worked with, a woman in a white apron came out of the back carrying a tray of baked goods. As cliché as this is going to sound, she took my breath away she was so beautiful. She was about five seven with blonde hair and big beautiful eyes—honestly, she looked very much like a young pre-surgery Pamela Anderson. I was completely taken away by this woman, and I can truthfully say that never in my life had I ever experienced a connection like that with anyone, especially a complete stranger.

As it turned out, that night, after crawling into bed and falling asleep, I dreamt about her. When I awoke the next day, I knew I'd be foolish to pretend that the universe hadn't given me a sign, so I knew I needed to do something about it. I remember asking myself that morning where I was even going to start with all this because, well, I didn't even know her name.

That morning at Tim Horton's while I was waiting for my coffee at the counter, I inquired to one of the staff if they could assist me in putting a name to this mystery woman I had seen working there the day before. After providing a brief description, I found out not only that her name was Marcy but that she was scheduled to work there again that day. It was then and there I decided to set a plan in motion.

I was facing a time crunch if I wanted to avoid being late for work that morning and so I ran—literally ran to my truck—and drove from Tim Horton's over to the local Safeway and ordered a dozen red roses from the floral department and arranged for them to be delivered to Marcy at Tim Horton's that day during her shift. My plan was that each day I would send her another dozen red roses and a card that would reveal another clue to my true identity until such time she discovered who I was.

Unfortunately, the gig was up quickly that first day and as I walked into Tim's Horton's in the afternoon for another coffee, I watched the staff member who had provided me Marcy's name walk over to her and whisper in her ear that the person who had inquired about her name that morning was in fact now in the building. It didn't matter. I still went to Safeway every morning after that day and ordered Marcy a dozen roses for delivery. After five or so dozen roses made their way into her hands, she finally gave me her number, and we planned a coffee date. As time went on, things between Marcy and I became more serious and we started dating.

Unsurprisingly, Ashley did not approve of Marcy whatsoever and, therefore, felt the need to insert herself into the equation the only way she could in order to try to control the situation—by placing restrictions on my time with Josh and Edward and making access to them difficult. I'm going to speculate here and suggest that her endgame with all this was to simply play Marcy off against the kids in hopes that guilt and frustration on my part would ultimately end our relationship.

It all started with Ashley voicing concerns to me that she had regarding my behaviour since I had met this new love in my life. She claimed I had started using alcohol, and she was sure there must be drug use in there as well—apparently, I was putting on weight, and according to her, that could be the only reason. I'll admit my social life at that point in time was definitely a lot busier than it had been in previous years, but I certainly wasn't doing anything illegal, and even during the lifestyle change I had going at that time, I was still maintaining all my responsibilities and commitments to my kids and to my employer.

As I've said before, she loved preaching to me, and this was a classic example of her doing just that. By this point Ashley had already had three or four different guys come in and out of not only her life, but the kids as well, yet here she was with the guff to voice her concerns to me about someone who had come into my life.

It became evident quickly that she was grasping at straws, anything she could do to control the outcome of what was happening in my life. But I had no intention of letting her have any control or influence over my future under any circumstances. It was shortly after these alleged concerns she had voiced to me that she started making changes to the parenting agreement we had in place. The first variation was a big one: she decided that she would keep Josh and Edward throughout the week.

I remember that being very difficult at first. It was a tough situation to learn to be in, and one in which my hands were completely tied. It felt like a pretty helpless, hopeless time. I guess in the back of my mind I knew this was probably a better arrangement for the kids—as opposed of being dragged between two households week after week, but it was really hard because I knew they were under Ashley's care for the wrong reasons.

We didn't have anything written in stone from a court yet at that time, and due to the design of the family law system, there wasn't much I could do about the changes Ashley had made. At that point, my time with Josh and Edward dwindled to weekends and they were now under her care and influence twenty-four hours a day. She was calling all the shots at this point, a pre-cursor to what she was going to do so many times over in the years to come, namely, starting to use the kids to get what she wanted for herself.

As it turns out, I wasn't the only one with love on the horizon, Ashley also had someone come along who wanted to take things to the next level. This is where that jackass I spoke of a while back came into the picture, and this is where things started to change and eventually get to a very ugly point.

His name was Dave, and I actually got along with him at first. I had no reason not to. He seemed like a pretty decent guy, he liked kids, he seemed funny, I can honestly say that I didn't mind the guy at all. He paid me respect, and I did him the same courtesy, there was absolutely no reason in the world at that time not to. Josh and Edward seemed to like him, so really, what more could I ask for under the circumstances?

Once Ashley and Dave had moved in together in early 2006, my sister Carol had started to go visit the kids a couple times a week at their place just so she could stay involved, and this was really the only glimpse I had into the daily lives of Josh and Edward, which as it turned out, wasn't a pretty picture. There were so many little things being instilled in the kids minds during those times, the kind of thing that any parent with half a brain would never want their children learning. As an example,

I remember Carol being completely beside herself, telling me how Ashely and Dave weren't allowed to have pets at the place they were living (but they did) and how she had witnessed them instructing the kids to lie about it if the landlord came around asking. Still blows my mind to this day. Teaching kids to lie at a young age. That's what she was doing.

Carol bore witness to many conversions between Ashley and the kids where she would ask them questions regarding whether they wanted to live with me or her, or who they liked better—me or her. Questions that no kid should ever be asked or expected to answer for that matter. When Carol would raise the question of the effects the instability might have due to all the moving around, Ashley would respond insisting that she had asked Josh and Edward and they said they wanted to move.

These conversations were just ridiculous.

I know these were tough times for Carol as well. No one was more concerned about all the events that were unfolding around the kids than Carol was, and that's the truth. She only ever had the best interest of the kids in mind. This whole process would prove daunting for her as well.

It was around this time I had the first official court date regarding child custody and the parenting agreement. At that point we'd still never been to court to get anything in writing officially. I didn't fully understand at the time that, once complete, these documents were written in stone and nearly impossible to change. Unfortunately for me, I wasn't focused and fully engaged in this first round of legalities surrounding my kids when I really needed to be, and that ended up working against me in the end.

The high stress and worry over what was happening in other areas of my life had consumed me and had drawn my attention away from this court date, which was a huge blunder on my part. I was facing a financial crisis at the time and was struggling to find enough money to cover the expenses I had to pay. I was literally weeks away from losing my house in Gibbons, and I didn't know what I could do to reverse any of it.

Truthfully, the reality of everything that was happening in my world at one time was just too much. I don't think any human being could have functioned properly under the amount of stress I was under at that time, and I know I certainly couldn't have taken anything more. I wanted to give up, I really did. It was hopeless. I still get anxiety to this day even thinking about how I was feeling those days. It was during this time that the court documents for this initial court hearing were supposedly sent my way, documents containing all the granular information regarding the details of my case including dates, times, and locations.

To this day, I honestly have no recollection of ever receiving any documents. I'm not saying I *didn't* get them—I mean I suppose I must have—I just have no recollection of ever seeing anything in writing about it. The stress of everything that was happening had taken a huge toll not only on my mind and my ability to process information, but also my ability to properly plan and manage the things that were happening around me.

It was a double-edged sword.

To this day, I can only speculate that it was all the stress that ultimately led to me missing that court date. I do vaguely remember a phone call from somebody about it at one point, but I honestly don't even remember what that conversation was about. I can't even remember if that was before the court date or after the court date for that matter. So it came and went, and no one was there to represent me—not even myself—and because no one was present, Ashley was awarded everything she had requested: full-time custody of the kids during the week with my access set to every second weekend and (more to the point) a child support payment set at eight hundred dollars a month.

It was evident to me, from that point forward, that I had clearly lost control of my life and needed to step back and make a plan before I did anything else.

Four

I knew changes had to be made, and those changes had to happen now. I started by making a list prioritizing the most stressful pressing issues I had—from biggest to smallest—and went from there. The fact I was now merely days away from losing my house was the single biggest issue I was facing.

With nowhere else to turn, I ended up having to ask my parents if they could help me out with the funds I needed to prevent the foreclosure on my house. I wasn't proud of this, of course, so naturally that was a difficult phone call to make. When I did finally scratch together the nerve to make the call, they weren't home anyway, so I just left a message on their voicemail, detailing what was going to be happening over the next few days in my life if I couldn't square things up with my mortgage.

I had already been to the bank to discuss the details regarding the foreclosure, and it was clear from that discussion I didn't have a hope in hell of ever coming up with the money required in the time frame required. Lucky for me my parents agreed to help by lending me the money I needed so I could settle things up.

Once things had been cleared up at the bank, I wasted no time getting my house on the market. For me, this was a necessary thing to do for more than one reason. First off, I couldn't afford to live there by myself; and secondly, things with Marcy and I were starting to take flight, and I had no intention of trying to start a new life with a new person in a place that represented a different time and a different life.

Everything Marcy and I were going to accomplish together had to be done from the ground up, together, and I knew that. Luckily for me the house sold relatively quickly, and before I knew it, I was packing up my shit and getting the fuck out of dodge. I had found a very nice condo in Fort Saskatchewan located near Josh and Edward, and the fresh start it would provide for me was very much needed.

With the money I had left over from the sale, I had enough to reimburse my parents what I had borrowed from them to avoid the foreclosure, plus cover the costs of my move, my damage deposit, and a months' rent at the new place. It was difficult knowing I was going to have to take a huge step backwards in life in order to move ahead.

I also knew that, due to the credit issues I now had, being able to purchase another house was something that was years into the future. Nonetheless, I felt a burden lifted from my shoulders the day that I closed the door on that house behind me for the very last time. Even just leaving that shitty little town for the last time was very therapeutic for me.

September of 2006 also marked Edward's first day of kindergarten at the same school Josh attended in Fort Saskatchewan. As with many other differences that were present between Josh and Edward, routine changes such as this proved much more difficult for Edward. I was thankful both he and Josh were in the same school to help comfort him during these times of change.

It was in around this time that my sister Carol moved away to the U.S for about a year. Her boyfriend Henry was in the final stages of a medical internship that had been underway for over a decade. He was going to the U.S to acquire training and knowledge in some very specialized areas, and so naturally Carol went along with him. It was a pretty cool opportunity, and I would have done the same thing of course if I were her.

It was tough for me when she left though. I'm not super close with my parents, and most of the family had migrated to British Columbia to start a new beginning following an unfortunate family event that had occurred a few years previous. Due to work related commitments, most of my closest friends were gone ninety percent of the time, so other than a few new acquaintances I had made—including Marcy, of course—I felt pretty isolated at times. I was still very much getting to know Marcy's family and the people in whose circles she ran.

I guess I was just out of my zone a bit because of all the new things I was experiencing, and the one person I really confided in was leaving for a while, and it felt weird because we had always lived fairly close to one another. In reality, I really wasn't alone, but it certainly felt like it at times.

Along with the other new changes I had recently been implementing in my life, I had also decided at that time to seek employment with a different company as well. At that time, I had been using a company vehicle for the past three years or so, and I didn't actually even have a personal vehicle anymore, so getting a vehicle lined up was a high priority at that time.

A good friend of mine ended up finding a decent used car at a lot for me, so I bought it. Unfortunately when I went to insure that car I opted out of the extended coverage for fire and theft for the first time since I started driving at sixteen years old—and that was something that would come back to bite me in the near future. I'll get to that shortly.

All in all, I felt I was on the right path to getting things back on track in my life. I felt like I could breathe a bit again, and as destiny would have it, a change in Marcy's living arrangements had led to her moving in with me, and I was ecstatic about her being the first thing I would see every morning when I opened my eyes. Things between us moved quickly, and I knew for the first time in my life, I had found the person I actually wanted to go all the way with and marry and spend the rest of my life with.

In April of 2006, only six months after I had met her, I asked Marcy if she would marry me. I know, crazy right? I know that's what a lot of the people we knew were saying about how quickly things were moving between us, but I just knew somehow, without a doubt, that this was real and not something I needed be scared to proceed with.

After accepting my proposal, Marcy and I set our wedding date for August of 2007 and sent out our wedding invitations shortly thereafter. From that point until the wedding the following year, Marcy was busy making preparations for everything and loving every minute of it.

Five

Unfortunately, the drama between Ashley and I had not changed at all. As a matter of fact, the drama was getting worse. Now that she had the kids full-time, the erratic behaviour she had always shown in the past had been kicked into high gear. Ashley had made mention to me that she had started both the kids on medication after both had apparently been diagnosed with ADHD. I have no doubt she was legitimately given the ADHD diagnosis, but I'm positive she only provided information to the doctor that supported that diagnosis.

Sure they were hyper, especially when they were together, but so what? They were kids. I'm positive if those doctors could've had a glimpse into what a day in the life of those kids looked like, they would have diagnosed the problem being a direct result of their home life and not a chemical imbalance.

At four and six my sons were entirely products of their environment.

All the instability she had introduced into their lives was starting to affect them, and that's all. Ashley was a firm believer that if there was any problem with the kids at all—whether it be behavioural, attitude, low marks in school, whatever the case was—there was a pill manufactured that could correct it.

My experience with every medication she had them taking was that they did absolutely nothing for the kids other than introduce weird side effects. I didn't see any change in behaviour or attitude because I don't think there was anything wrong to begin with. They were just normal little kids being just that. They didn't need to be on mind-altering medication because their mother felt that they were too much work and didn't want to deal with them. All this medication was one of the first red flags I picked up on after Ashley had taken full custody of the kids.

The accelerated moving was the other. I swear almost every single time we went to pick the kids up it was from a different address. They moved constantly. Sometimes they would move into a place that wasn't even big enough to house the amount of people that would be living there. They were literally moving every couple months. I mean, I get it, people do move, perhaps for a better job opportunity, a better location, an upgrade to their house (or perhaps a downgrade), cheaper rent, closer to a school, maybe an extra bedroom, whatever.

But Ashley moved for unknown reasons. There was never any rhyme nor reason to it. Looking in from the outside, Josh and Edward's lives appeared chaotic, and from the inside I'm sure it was much worse than that even. Some of these moves even found them in different towns in the surrounding areas of Fort Saskatchewan where the kids were still attending school.

It was with these out-of-town moves that it soon became evident that transportation was going to be the next big issue we were going to have. Ashley claimed that because I was now the "secondary" parent in the equation, it was my responsibility to provide all transportation for Josh and Edward, including any driving costs incurred relating to my time spent with them.

She refused to drive.

If I wanted to see the kids, I'd be driving both ways, or I wouldn't be seeing them. Any parent who genuinely cared about the overall well-being and development of their children would undoubtedly push for them to have a relationship with the other parent, especially if that parent wanted to be involved.

Ashley couldn't have cared less if Josh and Edward ever had contact with me again, so I really had no choice but to do all the driving if I wanted to be involved. It wasn't really a big deal at that point, but it certainly was going to be. At that time, it was just another piddly little thing for her do to try and inconvenience me in any way she could. I had to tolerate a lot of stupid shit from Ashley over the years just so I could stay involved with my kids. Either way, I'd have to put that fight on the back burner for the time being as the financial crisis I had been dealing with up to this point was back for round two—only this time the hurdles would be even greater.

During the time I had been dealing with the financial aspects of the potential foreclosure on my house, I had also defaulted on payments to another creditor who at that time had been granted the collection of the funds I owed via garnishment through the court system. This had all happened in the background, under the radar of course, so when I was served a court-ordered wage garnishment from my boss, I didn't really know what to say even. It was really awkward to have him hand me that piece of paper, look me in the eye, and verbally inform me that I'd been served. I feel bad for him to this day that he did have to serve me because I know that really put him in an awkward position that day.

Just like that, I quickly realized that any control of my life that I thought I had regained was once again gone, and if I thought the last go around I had with this financial business was tough, this round would prove nearly unbearable. Between the wage garnishment placed on me by the creditor and my child support payment, I was left with under two hundred dollars every two weeks to try and survive on.

The first thing I did was to sit down and tell Marcy what was happening with me financially. I certainly wasn't hiding anything from her about it, financial stuff just wasn't something that we had ever discussed in detail at that point. I was embarrassed about it, of course, and a bit uneasy as well because we were still very much in the early stages of our relationship, and I was worried she might opt out of taking things any further with me in favour of finding someone who's life wasn't a complete fucking disaster as mine must have appeared at that time.

The outcome of that conversation when we did sit down and talk was nothing at all what I had expected.

She told me that she'd never had money growing up, didn't have money now and that money really didn't matter to her anyways. She told me we could figure this out. It was a little over a month before I finally got about a half paycheck or so, and around the six-week mark before I actually received a full paycheck again.

Unfortunately, by this time, we were already at the stage of receiving notices in writing from the landlord that, due to the fact we were two months behind on rent, eviction was inevitable if the arrears weren't settled. We knew this was coming. Previous to the written notices, we'd be sitting at home and suddenly there would be a knock at the door, and it would be the landlord wanting to discuss the arrears on my account.

We had no choice at the time, with virtually no money coming in on my end and Marcy working a dead-end job at that time, what could we really do? We still had to eat.

We would mute the TV and remain silent inside the suite until the landlord would finally give up and go away.

It was a horrible thing to have to do and a horrible way to live. I hated it. I started using the stairs, and I avoided the elevators and the main lobby at all times to avoid running into the landlord. To my dismay, as I was trying to slip out of the building one day, I ended up bumping into her anyways. She was in one of the stairwells that I commonly used to enter and exit the building. So we went down to the office, sat down, and had a discussion about the issue at hand, namely, the unpaid rent.

To my genuine surprise this actually turned out to be a good productive talk. She was pretty cool I must say. She was as understanding as she could be on the issue, considering I was the one who had created the problem. She was more than willing to help try and find a solution to get things caught back up including putting off her boss as long as she could to try and buy me some time. I remember that she actually commented to me during our conversation that day that something in her gut was telling her that this type of behaviour wasn't something I was typically prone to.

As it turned out, at that time, an opportunity that had presented itself to Marcy and I was nearing completion, and it was through some hard work, long hours, and perseverance that we were successful in coming up with one extra month of rent on top of our ongoing rent payment to put against the arrears. Then to help us out, the landlord actually took our damage deposit, which was equivalent to one month's rent, and used that to pay the other month of arrears that was outstanding, which brought us up to date again with our rental agreement (less that required damage deposit). Things were looking like they were going to be alright.

Those were the toughest times financially that Marcy and I would ever see together, and there was nothing we'd face in the future financially that we couldn't handle after that.

Six

During this same time, Marcy had landed a much better job, and she had everything set up and scheduled to start a couple of weeks down the road. On the day she was scheduled to start that new job, we headed out in the morning to go to work as per our usual routine, and as we walked out into the parking lot, we were greeted by an empty stall where we were pretty damn sure we had parked our car the night before.

It was gone.

Someone had stolen it during the night. There was no trace of it. As it turned out, these series of events assured Marcy was going to be late on her first day at the new job. This is where I go back and explain the comment I made before about how, for the first time since I had started driving at sixteen years old, I had opted out of the extended coverage when I insured this car.

Cheap bastard, that's all that can be can said about that.

There was never a payout for the car because it wasn't covered for fire and theft. I notified the police department, and did my police report, but it's unlikely a fifteen-year-old economy car was something they planned on exhausting many resources looking for. So now, here we were without a vehicle again, and we certainly didn't have the money to buy another one.

We were very fortunate that Marcy's brother, Randy, had a car that he had recently retired that he gifted to us to get us by in this time of need. It actually was a decent car, and it would serve us well for the time being anyways.

A couple days after our other car was stolen, I received a call from the reception at the company I had recently quit, regarding a construction crew that was servicing a new subdivision on the south side of Edmonton. They had found my name as well as the name and number of said company on the separation slip provided to me when I left the organization. Someone on the construction crew had called them looking for me, and they, in turn, had contacted me to relay his name and number and let me know that he needed to speak with me about something.

When I called him, I was informed there was a large pile of my stuff laying in the middle of their construction site. It was the contents of our missing car. So I drove to the site and there everything was laying in the mud. The car seats, all my CDs, papers… everything was scattered in a giant puddle of water and mud. That pissed me right off. Taking the car was one thing, but it wasn't necessary to throw my possessions and my car seats and kids' toys in the mud. They could have left them in a pile somewhere out of the mud.

So I picked everything up, brought it all home, cleaned it up, and waited for the car to turn up. It never did. We actually never heard anything about it ever again. It just vanished, I guess.

But we had wheels again, thanks to Randy, and that was getting us by. However, happily ever after seldom stayed long with Marcy and I it seemed and as we were leaving the grocery store one day, shortly after we started driving that car, when we went to put the car into gear, the linkage that connects the shifter to the transmission broke, meaning we could no longer change gears in our car.

We were still very much trying to catch our breath financially at this point, after the ordeal we had just went through, so we couldn't really afford to get it fixed at that exact moment in time.

We did discover though that we could still switch the gears on the car manually, but that required opening the hood to do so.

This whole process must have looked ridiculous to bystanders.

If we had to back out of a stall or something, that would require multiple steps. One of us would have to get out, open the hood, put it in reverse, close the hood, let the other person back up, then open the hood again, put it in drive, close the hood, get in and go. The bigger issue with this was when one of us was alone with the car.

At that point you'd have to start the car, put on the e-brake, open the hood, put it in gear, close the hood, get in the car, take off the e-brake and then start driving, and that was only if you were driving forward from where you were parked. Having to back up first while alone was an even bigger nightmare. As Marcy and I only had one vehicle that we shared during that time, whoever was driving it to pick the other person up from work would have to hope like hell they didn't wind up in an emergent traffic situation that required a change of gears before picking the other person up.

The process of getting the car mobile by yourself regardless of direction was certainly a dangerous situation, and I found out just how dangerous after work one day.

I was getting ready to go pick Marcy up from work and I had taken all the steps to get the car moving as I mentioned above. It was early fall, slightly on the chilly side, and so the engine was revving higher than usual as it was warming itself up.

When I went around the front of the car to manually put it in the drive setting, it actually overpowered the e-brake, and I was nearly run over as it rolled forward. Then like an asshole, I had to run down the street after our car trying to get back into it while it was rolling away and get it stopped before it plowed into the cars parked down the street from it.

That is when we deemed it necessary to get a wheel chock and an appointment booked to get it fixed—before someone got hurt or killed. Marcy's stepdad who is a wealth of resources, lined up an appointment with some connections he had to get the repair done on our car for a really good price. I think he really called in a solid for us on that one.

As things would always seem to go with us, though, just as we would resolve one issue, another one would always pop up.

As it was to turn out, the peace we had recently made with the property management company was about to change again as well. The condo complex had been sold and taken over by a new organization and with that transaction came new eyes to an old issue. I received a phone call from the new property managers office to discuss the fact that they had no damage deposit on file for us and that they required one... *immediately.* Because our previous landlord had utilized the damage deposit to cover off the one month of rent that was still outstanding at the time as a favour to us, they were correct in their findings that there was no damage deposit in place.

There was no way we had the ability or the resources at that time to repeat the process we had used the last time to overcome this same obstacle, so we made the decision we'd have to move somewhere where the monthly expenses were lower.

Seven

My sister Carol and her now-fiancé Henry had just recently moved back from the U.S a few months prior to Marcy and I making the decision that we needed to relocate into a more affordable place to live. Upon hearing what our plans were, Carol voiced her opinion to us that she really wanted us to consider moving into Edmonton where they resided. She was concerned (and always had been) about the commute Marcy and I were making every morning to get to work in Edmonton, and she wanted to eliminate that drive and the hazards that it presented to us every day especially during the winter months.

After much thought and discussion, we decided we'd give it a shot. The move into Edmonton would undoubtedly carry some advantages with it. The rent was nearly half the cost of the place where we had been living, and the commute we had always made wouldn't be necessary anymore. The worst thing about it, for me, was the fact that I'd have to leave Josh and Edward behind and I knew the distance we were putting between us and them would be really hard. Thing's like having Josh and Edward over for supper every Wednesday evening as we would typically do when we lived in Fort Saskatchewan would no longer be possible with the new location we were living.

So in 2006 we packed up and moved into an apartment in Edmonton about thirty minutes away from Fort Saskatchewan. It was an older high-rise type building, and our suite was located on the twenty-fifth floor. I was the one who went and had a look at the suite initially because Marcy was tied up that night, and after viewing it, I remember thinking to myself that I liked it.

To this day, I'm not sure what the hell I saw exactly when I looked at it. I could have sworn it was a nice apartment. I was horrified the day we took possession of it and I walked into it again. It was a shithole to say the least.

Poor Marcy moving in, sight unseen, wasn't too happy with me—and that's putting it nicely.

To this day I wonder if it was the stress of trying to find a place to live with a negative credit rating as I had at the time that drove me out of desperation to sign an agreement that locked us in to that apartment for half a year. We had filled out applications for a couple other really nice apartments that I know we could have lived in comfortably, but we were denied on them.

Again, this was a direct result of me with my credit rating at the time, and it literally had nothing to do with Marcy; she was just stuck on this ride.

Luckily it was only a six-month lease, but six months in that place was long enough.

Three or so months into our stay at the new apartment, Marcy and I were headed out the door on our way to work one morning. We got to the elevator and pushed the button. Typically, the elevator wait times in this building could get up as high as two, two and a half minutes depending on the time of day because it was a twenty-five storey building with only two elevators. That day we waited about ten minutes before the elevator doors finally, slid open and when they did, we were greeted by the building maintenance man.

He immediately inquired as to where our assigned parking was in the building. After informing him that we parked in the bottom level parkade, he informed us that it was currently under eight feet of water.

Yes, it was true, our car had been completely submerged in over eight feet of water over the course of the night and would never turn a wheel again. I called my boss that morning and had him swing by my place to pick me up for work, and as we were driving past the ramp that led into the lower level of the parkade where Marcy and I had parked our car the night before, the water level inside came up to the sidewalk. That water was at least eight feet high in that parkade.

The source of the disaster, as it turned out, was the water main that fed the building. It entered into the building in that lower level parkade, which the building management team had decided to keep at a minimal temperature, likely in an attempt to save money on parkade heating costs.

I remember you could always see your breath down there, and it was cold enough that the florescent lights were dim because they couldn't warm up enough to work properly. It was cold and dark down there. Both Marcy and I disliked having to go down there. For the next week or two after the flood, the elevators were shut down as well because water had flooded the pit, and the elevators had to be serviced because of it.

It was twenty-five flights of stairs to our unit on the twenty-fifth floor, and it was well over a five-minute hike to get to our floor. The big problem at this point, though, was not the excessive climb to our apartment every time we had to come and go, but the fact that, yet again, here we were without a vehicle. Our car was deemed a write-off by the insurance company, and as with any insurance claim, it was going to take time for them to get all necessary paperwork completed and cut us a cheque to buy another vehicle.

Marcy's stepdad wasted no time in locating an affordable replacement vehicle for us, and they lent us the money to buy it. We ended up getting an older minivan this time, and believe me it certainly wasn't much to look at, but her stepdad said he knew that this was a reliable vehicle, and in all honesty, we really didn't have a lot of choices, so we went for it. It was actually kind of embarrassing to drive around in, but nonetheless it did get us around, and I won't complain about that.

When the money did finally come through from the insurance company for the car we lost in the flood, we were able to reimburse Marcy's parents the money they had lent us. With the vehicle issue resolved yet again, we decided the time had come to refocus our attention on our living arrangements and make a plan as to what we wanted to do with that.

This apartment was very small. It only had one bedroom, and when Josh and Edward came over, it was a tight space for all of us to share. The other thing that always made me uneasy about living in that building was just the sheer height of it. We were on the twenty-fifth floor. I always kept that balcony locked, and I never once let the kids out there with or without me, but I was always uneasy they might wake up before me one morning or something and go out there in curiosity. They never did, but it was always in the back of my mind.

Then there was the fire scenario. I always wondered if there was a fire in that building whether I could get my family down twenty-five flights of stairs and out safely.

We were undoubtedly unhappy with our move into Edmonton, and we wanted to move back to Fort Saskatchewan where Josh and Edward were. The commute was also something Marcy and I had discussed. We'd come to agree that it was something we were alright having to do again every morning if we were to move back. Our strategy was to initiate the plans we had made when the contractual agreements of our lease had been fulfilled over the following couple months. Being gone from Fort Saskatchewan for six months was long enough, we knew where we wanted to be, and we couldn't wait to get back.

We started our search for a place to live and found a nice two-bedroom apartment. As per usual those days, due to my credit issues, I was worried we might not get the place, but I was pleasantly surprised when the landlord called to inform us that we had indeed been approved for the rental. I know all we were doing was renting an apartment here, but I was so happy the day we found out we were moving back I could hardly contain myself. All we had to do now was sit back and wait for the day to arrive, and then we would be back where we had longed to be since we'd left.

Eight

I remember when moving day finally arrived in the early spring of 2007; the sun was shining, and I was feeling pretty good. As much as I hated moving, I didn't mind this move because we were going back home to Fort Saskatchewan.

The day we moved into our new place, I think Marcy and I both let out a sigh of relief to be back. It was a very plain and generic apartment, but it had everything we needed including more space, and that alone made me feel much better. The fact we were now on the third floor of a three-storey building also made me feel better. The greatest thing of all about it, was being close to Josh and Edward again, although things between Ashley and I were still on the steady decline and living close to each other once again only seemed to amplify the frequency of the problems we were having.

By this point, her boyfriend Dave and I had now stopped seeing eye to eye as well, and the battle between them and I was about to begin. Dave's whole demeanour towards me had started to change, and I didn't know why. He was starting to step on my toes, voicing his opinions on things that quite frankly had nothing to do with him, and calling me out as a father.

As I was soon to find out, Ashley and Dave were now pregnant, and they had dreamt up some ridiculous vision that they could create their own perfect little family including Josh and Edward without me around to tarnish it. I believe his change in demeanour was an attempt to try and intimidate me into backing away and eventually just bowing out of the picture. They just wanted my money every month and that was it.

I guess if I didn't care about Josh and Edward, all I would have done at the time was walk away from them and make a payment once a month because, believe me, that would have been a hell of a lot easier. Here's the thing with me though: I'm not about taking the easy way out of anything, I never have been. This little vision her and Dave had dreamt up of me being absent and out of the picture, well, that just wasn't going to happen.

I had no intention of not being involved with my kids. In reality, me being out of the picture wouldn't have helped them achieve their goals anyway, as the relationship between Ashley and Dave was toxic in itself, and word of that reached me one day from an unlikely source. Ashley and Dave took up residence in a house right across the street from someone I worked with. I remember him coming to work one day and informing me that the police had been at Ashley's house the previous evening. There had been a domestic dispute at her house, and the police had responded to it.

Josh and Edward undoubtedly bore witness to whatever transpired in that house that night, and to be honest with you, to this day, I really have no idea what they experienced. I'm not sure if they witnessed an act of violence against their mother, or an act of violence committed by their mother—maybe they didn't witness anything like that at all. Regardless of what did happen that night, I do know for a fact they witnessed aggression, yelling, swearing, and arguing at a level where it was deemed necessary that the police be called in to control the scene.

The kids should never have been put in the middle of that situation to begin with. To this day I still wonder what kind of immediate and lasting impact that may have had on them. Did my kids live in fear of domestic violence after witnessing it? Was this even the first time they had witnessed it? If that type of abuse was present in Ashley's home even once, it likely occurred either prior to this incident or again sometime over the course of the following years.

One thing I do know is if there was any other domestic disputes that took place at her home, she would have gone to extremes to prevent me from finding out even if that meant coaching the kids not to speak of it.

As the months went by, Ashley and Dave continued moving around sporadically and dragging the kids everywhere they went and regardless of where that was—Marcy and I were still expected to pick up and drop off the kids from wherever the wind blew them that month.

I didn't worry too much about the excessive moving when the driving was only fifteen or twenty minutes each way, but as this tale will tell, transportation was going to become a major issue. Unfortunately, Marcy and I were starting to have some vehicle issues again as the van we'd been driving was starting to show signs that it may not have much life left in it.

As fate would have it, an acquaintance I had made on the construction site I was working at during that time had just recently bought his wife a new SUV, and he had her other vehicle up for sale. It was a really nice van. I asked him how much he was looking to get for it, and he told me he wanted six thousand dollars for it. Marcy and I didn't really have the money at the time anyways, but out of spite and just to get a rise out of him, I offered him four thousand.

He laughed about it and not-so-politely declined my offer.

About a month or so later, he approached me one morning on site and asked me if I was wanted to buy the van from him or not. I asked him again how much he wanted for it, and this time he told me thirty five hundred. I must say, his negotiating skills certainly weren't the best because I still would have given him the four thousand I'd offered him originally if he'd asked for it.

As it had turned out, because of an opportunity that had presented itself a few weeks earlier through long hours, hard work, and perseverance, Marcy and I had the funds available to us to buy it—and just in the nick of time. Literally the day I went and picked up our new van, the other one rolled its tires for the last time and was dead in the water.

The best thing about all this, though, was that we had finally managed to get ourselves into a half-decent vehicle. At long last, it seemed as though some positive things were starting to happen for us, and anything positive at that point in our life I welcomed with open arms.

Nine

As the months of 2007 wore on, and summer slowly crept by, our wedding day finally arrived in August and the time had come for us to take our vows. I would like to take a moment to make a statement here and go on record with this: Marcy is the only woman I have ever officially been married to. I really hate it when people refer to Marcy as my second wife because she isn't. This is the only woman with whom I have ever stood with in a church, at an altar, with a priest, before God, and said, "I do."

The day before the wedding, we were at the venue getting everything set up. Everybody was there to help out, of course, parents from both sides, our siblings from both sides, the wedding party—and Josh and Edward were there as well.

During the process of getting everything laid out in the venue, the kids were running around like maniacs doing their thing. They were five and seven at that time and in their excitement were going full tilt. As it turned out, in their rambunctious state, they were chasing each other around, and one ran one way, the other ran the opposite way, and without a chance to stop or even slow down for that matter, they ran into each other at full speed and ended up cracking their skulls together in the process.

This was a very serious collision that these two had.

They both had massive goose eggs on their heads, the bigger concern was Edward who had a goose egg sticking out of his forehead the size of a golf ball. I remember Carol had him lying on the floor in the bathroom, and when I walked in to have a look at him, I absolutely could not believe the size of the lump protruding from his head. It was alarming.

Luckily for all parties involved, my brother-in-law Henry being a doctor had a look at both the kids and determined they were going to live, although it certainly didn't look like it. It was pretty obvious from that incident that the pictures the next day with the kids would not be as pristine as we had anticipated.

With absolutely no surprise to me whatsoever, when I opened my eyes and looked out the window the next day, it was raining like a motherfucker and gloomy as hell. Now add some wind into that equation, and you've got yourself a good old-fashioned shitty day outside. As if that wasn't bad enough, I had a massive pimple that had flared up overnight on the left side of my bottom lip. You can clearly see it in most of my wedding photos.

As for my Marcy that day, though, well, she was breathtaking to say the least. I can't even put it into words. She is the most beautiful woman on this planet, and in truth that's an understatement. What a fantastic day. Fun was had by all, and I'm not just saying that because it was our wedding either. It just had this vibe about it that I've seldom experienced at a wedding. It felt great.

Other than one groomsman who made an idiot out of himself, and one bridesmaid who made an ass out of herself, the night went without a hitch. In truth, it was a truly magical day and one I am quite fond of. I don't regret a thing, and if I could go back and do it all over again, I'd marry Marcy again in a heartbeat.

A few months after we tied the knot, Marcy and I became pregnant for the first time. Unfortunately, the universe had another plan, and Marcy had a miscarriage a month or two later and we ended up losing our baby. This devastated Marcy to her very core. It was hard to see her so distraught, especially because there was nothing I could do to help her deal with what she was experiencing. I know she struggled with that loss for a long time and only time could heal that wound.

During this short time period that we were pregnant, we quickly made the realization that a two-bedroom apartment was no longer going to suffice for us with two kids every second weekend and now a baby. So Marcy began looking for something that would better suit the big change we thought we were about to have in our lives. As she was scanning the classifieds of a local newspaper one day, she came across an ad for an acreage for rent that was located about fifteen minutes outside of Fort Saskatchewan, straight down the road from a little hamlet known as Josephburg.

After the loss of our baby, we really didn't need the upgrade in our living conditions, but we were nearing the end of our current lease at that apartment anyways, and although it was a decent enough place to live, the freedom that living on an acreage could bring us was a very powerful draw. On top of that, I was playing drums in a little weekend garage band at that time, and hands down the biggest challenge for our band was trying to find a place where we could crank up the volume and not piss a bunch of people off in the process. I knew moving out there would alleviate that problem for sure.

I grew up on an acreage, and once it's in your blood, it's in your blood forever, and nothing feels like home except exactly that. I longed for it, so we went and checked it out, and it was a perfect acreage—I almost couldn't believe it. It was a newer house on a mature treed lot. And although it most certainly was out in the country, it had city water, asphalt right to the driveway, and garbage pick-up!

As we were soon to find out, it was an amazing place to live.

It was actually owned by a Lutheran church located on the same parcel of land right next door. The church typically utilized that house for their pastor, but in this case, the pastor at that time had his own house nearby and didn't need the one on site, so they opted to rent it out. We filled out the applications and awaited a response. A couple days later, we received the good news—we had the green light to move in at the beginning of the following month.

I'll admit, I was a bit nervous about it once we found out we had the place because the rent was higher than our current place plus there would be utilities on top of that now as well, but nonetheless something inside told me we needed to move forward with it anyways. So we packed up our stuff and moved out to that acreage. Marcy was a bit freaked out the first month or two we were there and didn't like it because she wasn't used to living out in the sticks.

Nothing but pitch black outside the reach of the exterior lighting, wildlife making noises whilst roaming around in the forest surrounding the house, and perhaps the greatest thing of all that comes with living in the country… being surrounded by complete silence. This house had three bedrooms, so now Josh and Edward would each have their own bedrooms again. This was the first time since I had sold my house in Gibbons a few years back that the kids would have their own rooms to sleep in, and that felt like a victory, it really did.

We very quickly came to love it there. It was a fantastic place to live. I always told Marcy that it must be on hallowed ground because there was just something about that place that was amazing. I couldn't put my finger on it, just something. I felt good there. I was content. I couldn't wait to get home after work every day. I felt at peace. That was the only place I've ever lived—other than my childhood home—where I felt like I was where I belonged. From a mental health perspective, considering many of the circumstances that were still weighing on me heavily, I was undoubtably coping the best I had in a long while with the peace that acreage introduced into my mind.

Even the never-ending drama with Ashley seemed manageable and less urgent during those times. With my newfound clarity, I made the decision that the time had come to start dealing with all the financial ghosts of my past. I had already let this sit too long as it was and I knew undoubtedly that this was going to be a big hurdle. So I called up the credit bureaus and had them mail out my credit reports. When the credit reports arrived and I had a chance to look over them, it was quite the mess to say the least.

Everything I had just walked away from was still very much sitting there waiting to be dealt with. I came up with a plan to begin the process of paying these creditors off one by one. It certainly wasn't going to be quick, and it certainly wasn't going to be easy, but then again how was that any different from anything else in life. Nothing was easy. It was going to take some pretty intense discipline to stay on target with this, but I knew if I could remain focused with it, I would eventually clear everything up, and then I could start the process of rebuilding my credit for the future.

Marcy and I shared the dream of one day owning a home together somewhere, and achieving that dream had to begin right here. As with any journey, it started by putting one foot in front of the other. We sat down and discussed the details of what I wanted to do with all this, and she agreed it was something we could handle and something that needed to be addressed. After making some phone calls, I lined everything up with the first creditor and initiated my plan.

As I would pay a creditor out in full, they would give me what they called a relief letter in return. This was a letter to confirm that it was me who had approached them with the intent to pay everything in full and that, after making an agreement with them, I had followed through until the end and there was no longer any outstanding balance on the account.

To be honest, I found all the creditors I dealt with throughout this process to be quite reasonable—in fact, most actually made a commitment back to me in good faith by knocking a substantial amount of interest off what I owed them. Each time I would successfully fulfill my obligations and reach the end with a creditor I would feel a weight lifted off my shoulders.

It felt pretty good to finally stare it right in the eye and address it at long last because this was a monkey that had been on my back for a long time. It was a financially tight time for Marcy and me in our life as husband and wife, but nothing that we couldn't handle together. If anything, like so many other things we had gone through together since our story began, it only made us stronger. After everything was paid up, I wasn't sure what the next step towards rebuilding my credit was going to be, so Marcy did some research and located a credit card company that offered one card that existed solely for the purpose of establishing or rebuilding credit. It required a deposit to be placed against the account; then they would issue you a card that could be used as any other credit card.

This was the start of me rebuilding things for the future.

Ten

It was around this time it became evident that Ashley's only agenda was money. She got eight hundred dollars a month and was loath to spend it on the kids. They would come over to our house literally with holes in their shoes and clothes that were too small—she simply didn't care about their well-being. There were so many times that Carol would take the kids to the store and buy them new shoes and clothes just so they didn't have to go school looking like that.

Marcy and I didn't have any extra money on top of the eight hundred dollars monthly that we were now paying in child support, and so to this day, I am still grateful that Carol and Henry had the heart to do what they did. They have literally spent thousands of dollars on clothing alone for Josh and Edward, and all that money was over and above the thousands of dollars each year Ashley was receiving that was designed to encompass those expenses in the first place.

Ashley would constantly request more money for things that she said I was responsible for. I wish now that I'd made myself more familiar with the granular aspects of the child support system back then and known what I was actually required to cover over and above my monthly support payment. As an example, she used to ask me every year for the school fees for the kids, and I would give the money to her. It wasn't until I lawyered up—much later—that

I was made aware that fees just like those were already built in and included in that monthly payment.

Claiming section seven expenses was the next thing Ashley had discovered and zoned in on. For those of you who are not familiar with the child support act of Canada, on top of the pre-calculated monthly support payment that you are required to pay by law, the parent whom the children reside with can request money for extracurricular activities. These are known as section seven expenses. The parents are supposed to make an agreement as to what extracurricular activities their kids will be doing based on what they can afford and go from there. In my case, according to legislated guidelines, I was supposed to pay approximately eighty percent of any section seven expenses over and above my base child support payment.

Ashley and Dave would text me all the time looking for money for different things claiming they were section seven related expenses and telling me it was my responsibility as the kids' father to pay them. I remember, one time, Dave had called me and said they needed a hundred and fifty dollars for gas for a tournament the kids were participating in the following weekend. Like I was their personal bank machine or something. Section seven expenses are supposed to be agreed upon in advance and backed up with receipts, not a phone call requesting funds every weekend. These constant requests for more money from me was beginning to cause more friction in an already tense situation and I was getting tired of it.

During this time, Ashley and Dave ended up moving yet again, only this time to an acreage about a half-hour drive one way from where the kids attended school in Fort Saskatchewan. I didn't fully understand why they would move so far away because, by doing so, they were now in a different school board district, and there would be no bussing available to get the kids to their school.

I confronted Ashley on the issue, and she informed me she would drive them to school every day and that Dave and her had, in fact, had a discussion on that exact topic, and made a commitment before moving they could get the kids to the school in Fort Saskatchewan every day. I was still unsure how any of that made sense and why they couldn't have moved to an acreage that was at least within bussing distance of the school, but more so than anything, I was genuinely concerned about the amount of time the kids would now have to spend on a busy highway especially during the winter months just to get to school and back.

Anybody who has visited this fine country during the winter knows that the roads here can be absolutely treacherous at the best of times—so why would Ashley and Dave needlessly endanger two small children every day by not thinking things through before making a move like that? It was definitely very concerning to me, but as with everything else, my concern was not Ashley's concern.

They didn't stay at this place very long anyways—I'd say maybe a month to six weeks tops—and then came the phone call that changed everything.

Eleven

My sister Carol called me one morning on one of my off weekends from the kids and was extremely upset about the information she was about to give me. She was worried that Ashley and Dave may have packed up and moved away with the kids. As I mentioned previously, Carol had befriended Ashley in an attempt to maintain her contact with Josh and Edward, and she had remembered a comment Ashley had made previously about potentially moving everybody to Red Deer which was where Dave's parents resided—nearly a two-hour drive one-way from Fort Saskatchewan.

Carol questioned Ashley at the time about the impact moving the kids away from one side of their biological family including their dad might have on them. Ashley told Carol that she had asked the kids and they said they were alright with moving away. Carol had chalked it up to mere talk at that time as there was no indication it was anything else, and I certainly don't blame her for that.

That morning when she called me, however, she said the phone number she had for the kids when she called was no longer in service. Carol was unable to verify whether they were gone or not because she didn't know where they were living at that time, so she called me to further investigate it. I called the number I had for Josh and Edward, and yes, just as Carol had said, it was out of service.

With no other contact numbers at which to reach them, I jumped in the van and took a drive to the acreage where they had been living, and sure enough, the place was abandoned. They were gone. I didn't know what to say or what to do. I didn't know exactly where they had gone or whether they had in fact even left the area or not at that point.

I had an idea of *potentially* where they may have gone from what Carol had told me, but that was two hours away, and I had never spent any significant time in Red Deer so the place was unknown territory to me. I'd only passed through it in my travels a couple times to stop for some gas and a coffee on the way to Calgary. I really didn't know what to do. I started by doing some research about it online and was quick to determine that, because Ashley did in fact have the lion's share of custody regarding the kids, she very well could be within her legal rights moving them away without telling me.

Within a day or two of discovering the kids were gone, I received an email from Ashley regarding the situation. She confirmed that they had indeed moved away to Red Deer where Dave's parents were located just as Carol had suspected. Josh and Edward had attended the same school in Fort Saskatchewan from day one up to and including that Friday, and on the following Monday they were in a new school, hours away from anything they'd ever known including me and the rest of their biological family.

In the email Ashley went on to claim that they had made the decision to move based on the *fact*—as she called it—that she had more support in Red deer from Dave's family then she did in Fort Saskatchewan with us. Josh and Edward had all the support that they could have ever needed right where they had always been, and that was an *actual fact*, not just some unfounded claim.

My speculation in all this was that Ashley and Dave had likely been in talks with his parents, and because they now had a child together, his parents may have wanted them to relocate closer so that they could be involved with their grandchild. I would understand Dave's parents, desire for that completely, but then I wonder if his parents were ever really given an accurate snapshot of what my family's involvement with Josh and Edward was. Probably not.

I would like to think Dave's parents entertaining the idea of my children moving away from me and the rest of their family only so they could be closer to their grandchild could only have occurred from Ashley and Dave painting a picture of my kids living with a deadbeat dad and an uninvolved family so it wouldn't matter if they did move. I would like to think his parents would have discouraged a move like that had they known all the details.

Then again, I didn't know his parents, I have never met them, so perhaps they didn't care what impact a move like this might have on my kids, maybe like all the other parties involved here they only cared about what it would bring to the table for them. This is where transportation became a major issue. It was now a four-hour round trip to pick the kids up and get back home, and that four-hour trip would have to be made twice on any given weekend we wanted to see the kids.

Ashley had made it clear she would still not be responsible for any of the travelling required on those weekends. So when it all began, Marcy and I would leave right after work on the Friday and we'd be out on the open road around four thirty in the afternoon. Around six thirty in the evening we would finally arrive in Red Deer to pick the kids up. We would typically stop to grab a bite to eat before jumping back on to the road home and by the time we were done eating, it was usually around seven thirty.

After making the two hour trek back home we would typically find ourselves pulling into our driveway at around nine thirty or so. Sunday would pretty much be a repeat of Friday. We would leave home about three o'clock in the afternoon and get to Red Deer around five in the afternoon. We'd drop the kids off and hit the road and typically end up back at home around seven in the evening. It was eight hours of travelling for Marcy and me each weekend.

It was also a tremendous amount of wear and tear on our van, a tremendous time investment, and a tremendous expense as we would average a fuel bill of a hundred dollars for gas each weekend we did that trip. And why? Because Ashley decided to move Josh and Edward away, and we had to pay the price for it. On top of all that, the highway we now had to travel on to get the kids was infamous for bad accidents, being commonly impassible during the winter, and for people driving like complete assholes on it. It was an aggressive highway to say the least.

We knew as soon as we started making that trip, during the winter, the highway would undoubtedly dictate our ability to get the kids on our scheduled weekends or not. It was clear that we wouldn't be able to keep up with the excessive driving for long because it was just too much.

It was also evident that this had now escalated to an emergency situation, and my sister Carol suggested we needed to start booking consultations with some lawyers and find out, if nothing else, what options we did have in all this. So she booked us two consultations, and we went in together to discuss the details with some different lawyers. Both of those consultations were with older gentlemen who had a tunnel vision when it came to custody agreements, child support, and what options they claimed there were in all this.

They really didn't even seem interested in trying. The common denominator we took away from those first two consultations was simple: there was no way we would be able to force Ashley to bring the kids back from where she had taken them. We were shit outta luck on that one. However, when Carol had started lining up our consultations initially, she had made mention of it to an acquaintance of hers, and she was given the name Sylvia Reeves whom this friend claimed was a real shark, and recommended to Carol we book a consultation with as well.

As it turned out, we noted each time we had mentioned Sylvia Reeves name in the presence of these other lawyers during our consultations, they all had comments about how she could be a pain in the ass, and that she was difficult and this, that, and the other thing. That was a message received loud and clear—we should definitely have a sit down with her and get her input on the situation. And that is exactly what we did.

On our initial meeting with Sylvia, we noticed that her take on all this was quite different from the opinions we had heard before from the other lawyers. Unfortunately, she was in agreement with what the other lawyers had already told us in terms of forcing Ashley to bring the kids back—that simply wasn't going to happen. She did, however, feel that putting an agreement in place that would legally require Ashley to at least provide transportation for half of all travel during my weekends was not only something that should be put into place, but something that needed to be put into place in order to protect my access to the kids.

It needed to go through the court system, and having said that, it had to be soon. It was clear this had been left as long as it could, and I was going to have to lawyer up and start the process. It was only ever a matter of time really. In the interim, Sylvia suggested that, before moving ahead with anything further, two things should happen first.

Number one, I needed to enrol and attend the parenting after separation course offered by the family law branch of the government. This course was mandatory before being able to proceed to the courts relating to issues regarding my children. As Sylvia explained to us, should the time come when we did need to employ her services the parenting after separation certificate was the first thing she would require.

As it turned out, I found the course to be a wealth of extremely valuable information that I still utilize occasionally today with my kids. So that was a night class held downtown at the law courts building. It was held over one or two evenings and was undoubtedly a positive experience for me.

The other thing Sylvia strongly suggested was for Ashley and I to plan a mediation session and try to come to an agreement amongst ourselves to address the issue at hand, which at this time was the excessive travelling now necessary to gain access to the kids on my weekends. I talked to Ashley about it, and she agreed she would attend the mediation session to talk about things as long as it took place in Red Deer. She also requested that Dave be present at the mediation as well. I had no issue with that—this way I knew Marcy would also be present in the room and could also raise her concerns about the situation.

When the day of the mediation arrived, we hit the road after work and pulled into Red Deer about an hour before the meeting. I had some anxiety about the whole situation. Truthfully I didn't really want to sit across a table from either Ashley or Dave and discuss how we were going to try and rectify a situation that only existed because of them and their lack of care in the impact their decisions had on Marcy and me.

We arrived at the building and we met the mediator, Ashley, and Dave at the door outside the room. It was immediately awkward, and I found myself wishing I hadn't even have tried this approach. Once the mediation began—as I had suspected—things escalated quickly. When we brought up the idea of splitting the driving between the two of us, Dave immediately voiced his opinion and went on to say that the eight hundred dollar a month child support payment I was currently making covered very little of Josh and Edward's expenses as it was, and that he refused to put any money into gas to get the kids to me.

Then he said I was a lousy father and that the time and effort spent getting the kids to me was a complete waste anyways. Less than five minutes into that mediation, Dave and I were standing toe to toe, but the mediator got between us. For the record, this is not typical behaviour for me. I have never wasted a minute in my life trying to solve any issue using my fists. However, as with anybody, back me into a corner, and I've got an ugly side too. It takes a lot to get it to come out, but Dave had been pushing that button for a long time now, so it was a quick burning fuse that night.

Truthfully, I'm glad things didn't go all the way for his sake. Considering the circumstances, he didn't have a hope in hell of winning that fight because I knew exactly what I was fighting for... my children. What was he fighting for exactly?

The mediator ejected Dave from the mediation process and then also asked Marcy if she could leave in order to keep the number of people on each side even. Marcy was telling me on the way home that night that Dave was walking out of the building in front of her after they were asked to leave, and he was swearing and kicking stuff while having a little fit. It was good for a laugh.

The remainder of the mediation lasted maybe another ten minutes and it was clear Ashley wasn't going to play ball, and I was done talking about it, so I pulled the pin and Marcy and I began our two-hour trek back home. It was a complete waste of time. Exactly what I thought it was going to be. It became clear that the only way we would likely be able to move forward now was by securing a lawyer and going to court.

In the interim, Carol had just entered into an email chain with Ashley regarding questions and concerns she had about the kids. For the record, Carol has always had a very prominent role in the kids' lives right from the day they came into this world, and she was absolutely within her rights to voice her opinions and concerns about her nephews. Her concerns were things such as what the impact might be on the kids being moved away from one side of their family including their dad, or how the kids being made to travel eight hours two weekends a month especially during the winter was adding an unnecessary risk to them, concerns of that nature. Stuff Ashley didn't like being confronted on and didn't feel Carol should have any say on.

This was something Carol did on her own steam to try to get some kind of peace of mind for herself. It wasn't something that I had put her up to because I wasn't man enough to confront Ashley and Dave myself. In his infinite wisdom though, Dave took that as an indication Carol was doing my dirty work for me. He took it upon himself to respond to the emails my sister had sent to Ashley. This is where Dave really started to step out of line, and it was obvious he had an inflated sense of his role with the kids and what his importance within all this was.

He responded to Carol and told her he wasn't sure why she was contacting Ashley with any concerns regarding the kids. He told her none of this was any of her business and that she was merely an aunt in all this, and therefore, she had no say in anything regarding the kids. That statement made my blood boil. Carol was a blood relative of these kids with genuine concerns for their well-being. What was he? Just another forgettable face, and nothing more. One of many temporary acquaintances that Ashley brought into the kids' lives that came and went over the years and nothing more.

He told Carol it was Ashley and he who were raising the kids now and that moving away was the best thing they could have done for the kids. He went on to say that I really had nothing to do with Josh and Edward anyways before they moved away to Red Deer, so it didn't matter. At one point, he actually referred to me as a sperm donor. I really couldn't be bothered to take any offence from anything this asshole had to say about me, of course, but when he attacked my sister that really pissed me off.

The emails between Carol and Dave went back and forth for a while covering different issues. He told Carol he didn't want to hear anything about what we might do from a legal perspective if some of these issues didn't get resolved until he saw a subpoena. At that, he ended the email chain, claiming that, as the visiting parent, all transportation of the kids was my responsibility, and he would not allow Ashley or their child to do any travelling whatsoever for my weekends of access as the roads were too dangerous.

He made it very clear in that email that it didn't matter if Josh and Edward had to travel on dangerous roads, he just cared about *his* kid in all this. So we employed the services of Sylvia and set the ball rolling.

Twelve

I ended up having to borrow the money to retain Sylvia's services from Henry and Carol, and when I say borrow, I mean I still haven't paid them back to this day for any of the stuff they've stepped up for over the years.

Sylvia wasted no time in getting things organized and quickly had a court date booked in Fort Saskatchewan to begin addressing some of the issues. When that court date did arrive, I took a day off work to go to court as well. I had never officially dealt with the court up to this point—and of course never with representation in place—so I didn't really know what to expect. I dressed up in my nicest suit, and Marcy came with me. Carol and my parents showed up as well, and there was absolutely no outcome that day whatsoever.

In a matter of minutes, another court date had been set, and Sylvia was out of the courthouse and on her way back to her office. It was at this time I was told that any court proceedings regarding child custody will always take place wherever the kids are located. So in this case that was a two-hour drive away in Red Deer and every kilometre of that trip both ways would have an impact on that retainer we put down.

In preparation of the upcoming court date, Sylvia had instructed us during one of our trips to pick up the kids that we needed to establish where the halfway point along the journey was.

Her plan was to ask the court to make Ashley responsible to meet us at that halfway point each time the kids were travelling between homes. My experience with all this court stuff moving forward would prove always to be the same; Marcy and I would spend a considerable amount of time locating documents that the lawyer needed, faxing things, dropping things off, and making phone calls, and attending meetings. For me it also meant constant worry and anxiety in the back of mind around how much money was actually left in that retainer the lawyer was given to begin with.

I was always scared Sylvia was going to call to tell me that the well had run dry. The money never lasted long. At three hundred dollars an hour, it doesn't take long to burn through a pile of money. On top of that, they charge you for absolutely everything you can think of right down to staples.

A few weeks later, the court date had arrived, and Sylvia was locked and loaded. She intended to get absolutely everything addressed and in writing so there was nothing left that Ashley could vary from or use as a loophole. She wanted to wrap this thing up tight. At the end of that court session, everything was laid out in black and white from the transportation to the division of all holidays such as Christmas and summer vacation.

Ashley was made responsible by the court that day for half of all the driving required to make the exchange on our weekends of custody.

That was huge for Marcy and me.

That instantly cut four hours of driving off every weekend we had the kids, and it cut everything else involved with it in half as well. Sure the amount of driving was still excessive, but in comparison to what it was, we were quite happy about the outcome. It was about as good as it could get considering the circumstances, and the travelling would now be fair. But that wasn't the only thing in all of this that was being looked at. My child support payment was also being looked at again—all this while we were dealing with this other stuff.

I'll take my share of the responsibility here for how all this went wrong, and it was simply because I wasn't fully educated and in the know of the child support policies or how certain things could affect me down the road. As it turned out, Ashley and I had not been exchanging our tax information annually as we should have over the past nearly three years. When my child support payment was calculated in court that day, based on the average of my income over the last three years, the payment increased from eight hundred dollars a month to eleven hundred dollars a month.

This payment was handed down to me at a time when I was lucky to get a paycheque that even had a solid eighty hours on it. That was a three hundred dollar a month increase in one shot, and something that was undoubtedly going to have a financial impact for quite some time into the future. So in a nutshell, we had spent the lion's share of the retainer Henry and Carol had kicked in to retain a lawyer. We were granted our request to have the travelling to access the kids evenly split between Ashley and myself—and my child support payment was increased three hundred dollars a month to an all-time high of eleven hundred a month.

Thirteen

It was evident, moving forward, that I was going to have to make some financial adjustments in my life so I could still put food on our table. With the new parenting order assigned to Ashley, requiring her to meet us at the halfway point both ways on our weekends of access, she was going to have prepare for substantial drive times, gas consumption, and wear and tear on her vehicles now as well.

It was about time for Ashley and Dave to be inconvenienced and affected by their decisions as well. Unfortunately, Ashley and Dave being forced to drive halfway had created a more dangerous situation for the kids than just being forced for hours on end onto a highway infamous for its deadly history. At that particular time, Ashley and Dave had a small truck, and when everybody was loaded up inside, there wasn't enough room for three kids with three car seats in the extended portion of the cab.

I remember on one occasion they had put Josh up front in the middle between them with only a lap belt on. No car seat. It made me sick to my stomach to see that when they pulled up. If they had been involved in a collision or a loss of control type situation while Josh was in the front strapped in as he was, he would have perished without a doubt. Funny, Dave had no problem putting *my* kids' life at risk, but he never in a million years would have put his own kid at risk by doing the same thing.

I told Ashley what they had done was illegal, and if they ever did it again, I would involve the police. To be honest I didn't really know what to do, or whether the police could actually do anything or not—or if they would even care—but I had to do something, even it was just an empty threat. This did actually rectify the situation; in the future they would typically leave their kid at home when they came to drop off Josh and Edward.

They would, of course, still try to find ways to be as ignorant as possible towards us regarding the driving. I remember one such time, where Marcy and I had made the now two-hour round trip (instead of four hours) from where we lived to the halfway point. When Ashley and Dave arrived, after we had grabbed the kids, they ended up following us all the way back to Fort Saskatchewan, where we had just come from. They were headed there for the weekend anyways, but they made us drive halfway regardless.

Just bare-faced ignorance. Any chance Ashley and Dave got, they would try to inconvenience us and make us spend money unnecessarily if they could—and then claim Marcy and I were the issue. This was behaviour that would continue well into the future.

The moving around that was so prominent when they still lived in Fort Saskatchewan was still very much an issue in Red Deer. That aspect hadn't changed at all. They moved at least five or six times during their stay in Red Deer, and this included multiple school changes which Ashley never once mentioned anything to me about. Due to the fact busing for schools is zoned—serving one school or another—when Ashley and Dave would move to a new location, they would occasionally wind up in a different school zone and the buses from that new zone wouldn't run to where the kids had been attending school. Because Ashley didn't want to have to drive the kids to school every day, she would simply enrol them in the nearest school serving their new location.

Because Marcy and I were so far away now and were only ever meeting at a halfway point to Red Deer, it became much harder for us to get a glimpse of what was happening day to day in the kids' lives, and I had no idea all this had been going on in the background.

Back on the home front, things for Marcy and I—for reasons beyond our control—were going to be changing as well. Upon returning home one day, we found a letter waiting for us on the door. When we opened it, we were met by a document stating that we had to vacate our little piece of paradise on the acreage and had been given sixty days to do so. It turned out the current pastor was going to be relocated to a church somewhere else, and the pastor replacing him would require the house to live in while running the church.

That was a tough day.

I remember feeling super disappointed knowing we had to leave that place. In hindsight, I still very much miss that acreage; it has a place in my heart that represents a paradise found during one of the most turbulent times in my life. It may sound weird I talk about a house like it's a long lost love or something, but if you've ever experienced finding the place you were meant to be—the safety and security that wraps around you like a blanket when you're there, and the feeling of absolute peace that reaches to every corner of your soul when you do find it—then you would be able to connect with me on this and understand why I feel the way I do.

Truth is, it was probably better it went the way it did.

We loved that place so much that it essentially kept us blind. We lived at that acreage for a year, and the entire time we were there, we were so perfectly content that we completely lost sight of the fact that we were paying rent and not accomplishing a damn thing in the process by doing so. If the church had never needed that house for anything ever again, we happily would have paid rent there forever, never realizing the mistake we had made in doing so before it was too late.

I knew we would be premature in trying to purchase a home at that time, from a credit perspective. Even with the credit-building card it was going to take time before there was anything showing on my bureau to indicate to creditors that I was, in fact, a reliable consumer they could trust to pay his bills every month. We were also premature from a down payment perspective as well.

As we were getting ready to start our search for a new place to rent, we were approached by Marcy's brother Randy and his wife Lyla and offered an amazing proposition. They had already talked about this between themselves—if we were interested, we were more than welcome to move into their house with them, free of charge, so we could concentrate on saving up a down payment to buy a house of our own. What an amazing thing for them to offer us. It didn't take Marcy and I long to agree that this was a once in lifetime opportunity we needed to take advantage of. The generosity these two extended to us at that time was instrumental in helping us finally get things together to become homeowners ourselves.

Fourteen

As sad as we were to be leaving the acreage, the future was now bright and carried a breath of excitement with it. We spent our final month there cleaning everything up really good and slowly moving all our stuff into storage for the duration of our stay at our temporary new home.

When the final day did arrive, we did our walkthrough with the landlord and said goodbye to her forever. I won't lie, the last time I drove away from that place I was pretty sad. So we moved in with Randy and Lyla and we began saving immediately.

We saved everything we could during that time, and it started to add up fast.

We were however very conscious of the fact that this was somebody else's house we were in, and we tried to leave as little of a footprint in their daily lives as we could. We would try and give them as much time alone as possible so as not to impinge on their personal time together. We would stay out until after nine most nights.

We made sure we bought our own food, and we tried to keep the house clean by doing dishes and cleaning the kitchen daily so they didn't have to worry about it. I know they certainly didn't expect us to do that, but we were just so appreciative of them for everything they were doing for us, it was the least that we could do. The only issue that came up was our weekends with the kids.

Randy and Lyla didn't have any kids yet at that point, and I know I certainly didn't feel comfortable bringing two kids into their home for the duration of a weekend and disrupting any routines that they may have had. So we decided the best thing to do would be to hang out somewhere else during the weekends we had the kids. That idea worked out better than I had originally anticipated.

My family didn't see the kids very often since they'd moved to Red Deer, so staying at Henry and Carol's or my parents' place offered them the chance to spend some time with the kids as well. So initially we would take them to Henry and Carol's for the weekend and just hang out there.

As it turned it though, Henry's parents had recently moved back to Edmonton and were needing a place to stay while they were waiting to take possession of their new home. So we started staying at my parents' place instead, located back in my hometown of Westlock. This was another long drive on top of a long drive, but that worked too.

BUT my parents travelled a lot, and so it wasn't long before there came a weekend where we really had nowhere to go with the kids. On those weekends, we decided we would simply make the full two-hour trek to Red Deer on the Saturday and take the kids out for the day.

This seemed to work alright as well, although it was a ton of driving and that was starting to take its toll on our van. We started noticing that on long trips that about an hour or so into a steady drive, we would lose one gear in the transmission. Almost like we lost the overdrive gear. Once the van had cooled down after having a rest for a while, it was good to go again until an hour or so later of steady driving. The problem with this was the consumption of fuel that would occur when we lost that overdrive gear. It would get really shitty mileage and the cost of the fuel for that trip would be substantially higher than normal.

I'm certainly not going to sit here and complain about the service that van provided to us for a good three years because it was pretty awesome. It never gave us a single issue before the transmission problem occurred.

One of the weekends we had driven out to spend the day with Josh and Edward we had decided to take them to a movie. The movie playing at that time was called *Monsters vs Aliens*. For those of you who haven't seen it, it's an animated kids' movie with a PG rating—as in parental guidance—and appropriate for anybody seven and up. After the movie, we went out for supper, dropped the kids off, and then Marcy and I started the long drive back home.

About halfway home Ashley texted me and told me that it was an inappropriate movie that we had taken the kids to, and that because of that, she was refusing us any further access to the kids until I smartened up. If you think Ashley had some type of justification in her statement, then watch the movie and then tell me what you think. The kids had a good fun day, and for Ashley that wasn't good enough. She had to try and put some kind of negative spin on it.

I think things were really starting to go sideways in her world and that her behaviour towards me was a manifestation of just that. The perfect little life and family Ashley thought she could have by simply packing up and moving away was not shaping up as such. Being so far way with so little contact with the kids, I had little to no insight as to what was happening behind closed doors. Communication between Ashley and I didn't exist, and even if there had been communication, it certainly wouldn't have been concerning things going wrong in her life and how that might be affecting the kids.

Fifteen

During the time Ashley had been punishing Marcy and I by forbidding any contact with the kids for having taken them to *Monsters vs Aliens*, there were some pretty serious issues unfolding at her place. It seems Josh and Dave had been having problems. To this day, I don't know the nature of those issues. All I know is Ashley and Dave decided they needed to take drastic measures to try and rectify it.

What they ended up doing was moving Josh out of their house and into Dave's parents' house. Ashley told me she had made the decision and that Josh could stay there until he learned some respect.

What a terrible thing to do.

To this day, I wonder how Josh must have felt being put into that position. To have your own mother cast you aside and send you away to live with people you hardly know because you're not getting along with her husband—it's fucking terrible. Being removed from your siblings, your house, even your own bed, and then being made to sleep in a strange place with strange people. How is that helpful whatsoever?

It was very sad, and when I found out what she had done, it wore very heavily on me. I would almost guarantee that Dave was glad Josh was out of the picture for the time being so he didn't have to deal with it. Any normal caring mother would never have subjected their child to such treatment. No way. In the event her children and new spouse were in conflict on a continual basis she would likely seek family counselling of some type. In the event counselling was unsuccessful, she would likely look to separation from her spouse in resolving the issue. Not separation from the child she brought into this world to appease her spouse.

Looking at it now, every single person in Josh and Edward's lives at that point were only temporary entities, and sadly that includes the two siblings Ashley eventually would have with Dave. I went in to see Sylvia about the situation regarding what Ashley had done sending Josh elsewhere to live, and she instructed me that I needed to call Dave's parents and talk to them about the situation at hand.

I remember being at home the night I called pacing back and forth in the kitchen being nervous about the call. I didn't know these people; I'd never met them. I didn't even know their names. On top of that, I didn't know how they were treating Josh or how he was getting along. I didn't know anything. Those were the thoughts in my head that gave me the courage to make the call. For the sake of his well-being, I needed to touch base with these people and make them aware that, regardless of what they had been told, I was very much involved with my kids, and how having one of them living there very much concerned me, and that I was aware and monitoring the situation.

So I dialed their number.

Dave's mother answered the phone initially, and I introduced myself to her. She was prompt in putting her husband on the phone to talk to me. I introduced myself to him and went on to voice my concerns regarding the arrangements. Dave's father seemed like a nice enough guy, but you can't get a good judge of character on anybody from a fifteen-minute phone conversation, so the unease I felt never went away during or after our little chat on the phone.

He said things had been getting heated at Ashley's house between Josh and Dave and that Josh had been moved there for a cool down period. He assured me Josh was being treated fairly and being looked after properly. That didn't mean a whole hell of lot to me to be honest. Why didn't Dave go stay with his parents then for a cool down period? At that point, I started calling Josh every night at Dave's parents place just so he knew I was there for him.

I entered back into talks with Sylvia at this time as I wanted to address the fact that Dave had made it clear he was refusing to allow Ashley to drive to the halfway point anymore during the winter months because she was pregnant and that was causing there to be significant gaps in us seeing the kids. Remember, Dave still had no issue with *my* kids being on those roads during the winter months, it was only once *his* kids were conceived that it became a safety issue.

Sylvia basically told me, as per usual, there wasn't much I could do about the situation. We'd have to wait it out and see where it was going to go from there. She did however present the idea that likely the best solution to end all this once and for all, was to utilize the services of a Greyhound bus route. This was not something that I was even the slightest amount interested in doing.

In fact, it terrified me to my core.

In July of 2008 a mentally ill individual stabbed and beheaded a fellow passenger on a Greyhound on a route from Edmonton to Winnipeg. The brutality of that attack wasn't going to be forgotten any time soon.

Because Ashley had moved far enough away that access to the kids had become difficult, I was now going to be forced to send Josh and Edward back and forth on a bus line with security so lax they couldn't even detect concealed weapons on the passengers utilizing their services. This was something I struggled to come to terms with. I knew Marcy and I couldn't do the drive the full distance back and forth to get the kids anymore. Eight hours a weekend was just too much driving, and our van had made it clear to us it wouldn't be able to stand up to the challenge that trip presented twice a month either for very long.

We had no choice.

If we were going to maintain our scheduled time with the kids, which was very important to all parties involved, then we were going to have to send them by bus. So Sylvia drew the papers up, and Ashley signed off on the idea. This little bus trip my kids now had to endure twice a month would mark the beginning of a terribly stressful time for me for the foreseeable future.

Sixteen

There were a few different Greyhound stops in Edmonton. The most questionable and sketchy of all these locations being the station in the downtown core. In all the years I had lived and worked in or around Edmonton, I had always steered clear of that area in general. Just the sheer demographic of it drew a lot of scary, questionable individuals to it.

It was a scary place to say the least. There were always intoxicated individuals there and people fighting, arguing, swearing and yelling. I hated it. I certainly didn't want my kids anywhere near that bus station if I could prevent it, so I inquired to the bus company as to whether or not I could drop them off and pick them up at a satellite location. There was a location on the far south side of Edmonton that—although presented a significant drive across the entire city to get there—would be the last stop prior to where the kids would get off when they arrived either in Edmonton or back home in Red Deer. This would have been ideal, but as it turned out, because Josh and Edward were underage, they had to depart from the downtown location which also doubled as the carrier's head office.

I had an ache in the pit of my stomach when I learned that piece of information and what that meant for my kids. I started making it a habit to grab their return tickets earlier in the week instead of the day they were going home. I found if I went to the bus station early in the morning, on like a Tuesday or something, there wouldn't be many people around, and I could get in and out quickly.

So typically, the way it all went down on Friday's was like this: Ashley would put the kids on the bus in Red Deer at around six thirty or so in the evening. I would wait around after work and do whatever to kill some time until the kids did arrive. They would have to stop at three or four places along the way before arriving at the downtown location in Edmonton, where I was waiting for them. They would usually arrive between eight thirty and nine fifteen in the evening depending on road conditions.

Because it wasn't possible, from the parking lot, to see when the buses were arriving, I would head into the bus station forty-five minutes early. The thought of not being there to meet the kids upon their arrival caused me severe anxiety, so I always went in early and waited by the door. Any of the time I spent inside that building I was on high alert. When the kids did arrive, I would quickly grab them, get them loaded them up, and get the hell out of there.

Then, on the Sunday, I would show up and get them loaded on the bus. As they were underage, they were required to sit right behind the bus driver, which made me feel a bit better. Although Josh did tell me a couple times that some bus drivers had allowed them to sit wherever they wanted once the bus was en route which I wasn't too happy about.

On one trip, they were sitting somewhere other than behind the driver—as they should have been—and they were likely messing around as kids have tendency to do, and some guy told them both to (and I quote) "shut the fuck up." Hard to believe anybody annoyed or otherwise would say that to a seven and an eight-year-old kid. Anytime the bus was arriving on my end, I was right at the front and centre of that line looking to verify they were sitting in the front of the bus.

When they would load up to leave on the return trip home, I would stand in that loading dock for a half-hour, even forty-five minutes sometimes, and just watch over them until the driver closed the door and drove away. Then filled with anxiety for the next three hours, I would wait for confirmation from Ashley that she had in fact received the kids in good order on her end.

The winter months were the worst with this arrangement.

There were many times the bus was well over an hour late due to road conditions. This would put my anxiety through the roof. I was always scared that something awful was going to happen, and my kids would be stuck right in the middle of it and I wouldn't be there to help them. I know that may sound morbid, but with the history of Greyhound and the reality of Canadian winter highways, it wasn't hard for awful thoughts like that to creep into my mind.

As it turned out, I ended up making friends with one of the ushers who worked for the bus line, and he was always helpful in alleviating the stress and anxiety I would suffer from when I was in the bus station. He would hang out with me and we'd talk about whatever. He would even go and get me updates on the road conditions and the likely location of my kids' bus.

I can't stress enough how much I fucking hated those times in my life.

Unfortunately, the busing arrangement was only going to get worse—but not for the reasons you're likely expecting.

Seventeen

On a more positive note, Marcy and I were cobbling together a down payment for a house, and we were quickly approaching our target number. My credit was also well on its way to reflecting a positive score, but it was still going to be a while before it would be an asset to us that we could use to buy a house.

My parents had even offered to co-sign, if needed, when we did find the house we wanted to buy. This was a huge game changer as well. All the planets were slowly starting to align, and with some help from both sides of our families, we were so close to achieving what we had set out to accomplish that we could taste it.

So began the search for our new home.

We were in love with Fort Saskatchewan when the house hunting began, but we were soon to discover that, due to an all-time high demand in the housing market and a super strong economy, the houses in Fort Saskatchewan were selling substantially above our price point. That certainly put a damper on the whole process.

Don't get me wrong, these were still exciting times, of course, but we were now going to have to look in alternate locations, where the house prices fit within our budget. It was while we were searching for our house that life changing news was delivered to us yet once again.

Marcy and I were pregnant.

It had been a couple years since we had gone down that road together, and although it was good news, Marcy was extremely nervous considering the outcome of her previous pregnancy. The search for a house became that much more important for us now.

We knew that once we did find the place we wanted to buy, we would still have to set up the nursery and the list went on and on. We were booking quite a few showings in different areas with our realtor, but we just weren't finding anything that even interested us in the slightest. These places were either old or run down or had weird floor plans—and some had really dark energy in them. I guess for the price point we were looking to spend, there just weren't a lot of nice places to be had.

Then one day, our realtor finally came across a house that fit the bill. It was a newer house, very plain, very small, but it was bright, clean, had good energy. Furthermore, out of all of the other places we'd looked at, it was the closet fit for everything we needed including the price. The only problem with it was its location.

It wasn't where we wanted to be.

It was located in a town called Morinville, a half-hour drive north west of Fort Saskatchewan. But its location was what really drove the price so that it fit within our budget. It wasn't out in the middle of nowhere by any stretch of the imagination, it was actually about fifteen minutes from the City of St. Albert located to the south. The issue with the whole thing was that I'm not a small-town kind of guy.

Both Marcy and I grew up in small towns, and the first house I had owned was in a small town. To be honest, I wasn't sure I wanted to live in a small town again, and then have to raise our new child in a small town as well. Having said that, neither Marcy nor I were fond of the big city either. We found we didn't like the hustle bustle that life there carried with it. Busy everywhere.

That's why we loved Fort Saskatchewan so much. It was a perfect balance between small town and major city. So we had to sit down and figure out what options we realistically had and what we were going to do. We agreed it wasn't a horrible town, it had some of the bigger food and coffee chains within it. Location-wise, it wasn't terrible. We knew from living around the area all our lives that this town had a very strong police presence known for keeping things very much in check. It was nice to know the community was safe.

We knew we wouldn't have to live there forever. This could be a steppingstone to eventually relocating to where we really wanted to be. After bouncing statements like that off each other for a while and coming down to brass tacks, we really didn't have a choice. We agreed we needed to go for it.

We had a baby coming, and we still needed to get set up and ready to go for when it did finally come into the world. So we called up the realtor and entered into negotiations on the place. It had been on the market quite a while at that time, which afforded us some bargaining strength, and in the preceding months, the market had cooled.

After some back-and-forth with the owners, we came to an agreement, and just like that we had bought ourselves a home. We did end up requiring my parents to throw a signature on that mortgage to gain approval on the financing, but we knew that was only a temporary arrangement as well. All that mattered was the fact we were in the real estate game at long last.

Eighteen

It was going to be six or eight weeks before Marcy and I took possession of our new home, so we used that grace period, while staying with Randy and Lyla, to just relax after all the hard work, long hours, and perseverance that had gotten us to where we were now. We started using the extra money we were saving with no rent, mortgage, or utility payments at the time to start acquiring the stuff we were going to need for our baby. Marcy and I were starting from scratch here.

By the time possession day of our house rolled around, we had pretty much purchased everything major required for a baby, and it was all boxed up sitting in the basement at Randy and Lyla's place ready to be moved. As with damn near every other place we had lived at to date, a very familiar problem had resurfaced yet again with our new home—there weren't going to be enough bedrooms to go around.

This house had three bedrooms, and up until very recently in our lives, three would have sufficed, but with our new baby on the way, we were going to need four bedrooms now no matter how we looked at. For the time being, when the kids did come over on our weekends, they would have to share a room until we figured out what we were going to do.

Luckily for us, this house did offer the potential to meet all our needs, it just needed a few dollars and some elbow grease thrown at it to unlock that potential. It had an unfinished basement, and that was exactly what we were going to utilize to overcome the hurdle of not having enough bedrooms this time around.

Marcy and I wasted no time after moving into our house to begin the planning and layout of the basement in such a way that made the best use of the space. It was a small house, and the basement was no exception; it was pretty tiny, but we were able to come up with a design that allowed us to create two bedrooms down there, a full bath, a small computer area, a storage closet, and a decent-sized open-concept media room.

Usually, before I attempt to build pretty much anything, I call in my dad, who happens to have some pretty solid experience in framing from years back when he was a young man. It doesn't seem to matter what I'm doing, anytime I get my dad involved with things, they always seem to go smooth. He has a knack for being able to make things work out. So that's what I did.

Marcy and I had everything laid out, marked, and ready to go, and so my dad and I went straight to building walls and standing them up. Six months into the basement development, we were in the drywall and taping stages and it was coming together nicely.

It was at this time Marcy gave birth to Michael, our first child, and life would never be the same from that day forth.

This was a truly exciting time, but deep down it still made me nervous. I knew that Marcy and I had done it right—we had a couple years of marriage under our belts now, our relationship was in a good place, we had recently acquired a home of our own, this little baby that just came into the world was surrounded by nothing but love and happiness. For me, raising children with Marcy, for many reasons and on many levels, was very important.

I had a very clouded view of what having children was all about, and without Marcy and our children, I would have missed the big picture. I can remember when Carol and Henry had decided to start having their kids, I couldn't quite comprehend at that time why anybody would want to put themselves into that position.

I know that sounds like a terrible thing to say, especially from someone who had kids at that time, but honestly all of my experiences raising kids to date had been shrouded in negativity in one form or another, and that was why I had the outlook that I did.

When you have someone who is deliberately going against you every step of the way—just for the sake of being difficult—it wears on you. When that someone constantly makes things as hard as possible just because they have the ability to do so, it wears on you. When that someone puts your kids in the middle of every single thing they possibly can, it wears on you. When that someone minimizes their contributions to your kids upbringing and then uses them, year after year, in any way possible, just to get at your paycheque, it wears on you. And when you're unable to do anything about any of it because the system of checks and balances *feels* like it's stacked against you, it wears on you.

Until the day I looked at Michael for the first time, I didn't realize how amazing it all really is. It provided me with clarity where none had existed for a very long time.

As it turned out, the journey Marcy and I were about to embark on together was going to undo the many beliefs that I had instilled in myself over the years due to the experiences that I had co-parenting with Ashley and our kids. It was a completely different adventure this time around, and I can honestly say that I have loved every single minute of it for nearly the last decade and counting.

Being on the same page with somebody with all the decisions regarding your kids really makes for a positive and fulfilling experience and assures that the kid's best interests will always be put first. When both parents work hard to provide for their children and to achieve other common goals between them, the results of that hard work in all aspects is rewarding beyond anything a person could ever imagine. Certainly more than I could ever have imagined.

Even after the absolutely horrible co-parenting experiences I had with Ashley and our two kids, in the end, I was given yet another opportunity to see how amazing these little human beings are—and without Marcy, that second opportunity would never have presented itself to me. I consider myself fortunate to have had that second chance to do it all over again.

Nineteen

Back at Ashley's, things between Josh and Dave had reached what one could only call the point of no return. Things had deteriorated to a level where there was essentially no going back. To this day, As I mentioned previously, I have no idea what the issues were between Dave and Josh, nor do I know the nature of the problems or how ugly things may have gotten between them. I don't really even know if it got physical. Believe me when I tell you I am the last person in the world who ever would have been given any of the details.

Ashley and Dave would have gone to extremes to ensure I didn't find anything out about the goings on at their residence. It was while all this was going down at Ashley's that I received a phone call from Josh one day. He was extremely upset. He was crying to the point where he was having a hard time even getting words out.

I asked him what was going on, and why he was so upset. He told me that his mom and Dave had decided that they didn't want him to live there anymore. It may sound like I'm making up a load of shit here, but this actually happened, and it was no empty threat. They genuinely wanted him to leave. To this day, it absolutely boggles my mind that any parent could do that to their child.

Josh was nine years old when all this went down.

They made a nine-year-old kid call his dad to ask if he could come live with him because he wasn't welcome. If things were so far gone that there was no hope that it was ever going to work between Dave and Josh—and Ashley had opted to stick with Dave over her own flesh and blood—then you'd think she would have at least communicated that to me herself. You'd hope she'd want to make me aware of what was happening and perhaps even ask for my input on the situation. You'd expect that she'd want to discuss the possibility of me taking custody of Josh directly. Not Ashely though.

The way Josh sounded on the phone that day still bothers me. I know that he didn't want to come live with us. I could even hear that in his voice, and I certainly didn't blame him for that. Even though we had stayed in very close contact with these kids over the years, and they knew us well and were comfortable around us, he didn't want to leave his mom and his siblings and move two hours away with me and Marcy. But he had no choice in the matter, and that was made very clear to him. From the day of that phone call, everything happened very fast.

Within a week, I was headed to the halfway point we had established to pick him up. Marcy and I had spent the previous week getting everything arranged to receive him on our end. We had to go to the school and get acquainted with the staff there, get him registered for classes, line up all his school supplies, and pay his fees for the year. This was in November, so on top of already starting a new school a couple months previous while still under Ashley's care, due to her moving around, he now had to start yet another new school just two months into that year.

On a more positive note, one thing that I can tell you is that the kids that he met in this new school were the same kids that he graduated with eight years later. The only school changes he would ever make again were the mandatory ones that everyone makes together from elementary, to junior high, to high school.

We also had to make preparations at home during that week for his arrival as well. We did have a bedroom available in the house that he could use—the only unfortunate thing with that though was the room was located right next door to Michael who was still waking up three or four times a night to eat. It was going to have to suffice though in the interim until the basement was completed at which point everyone would have their own bedrooms once again.

When the day arrived to pick him up, I knew it wasn't going to be an easy day for him. Josh and Edward had endured so much together over the years that they had a really strong bond—they knew they could always depend on each other. That bond was so strong (and still is) it will likely last their entire lifetime, and pulling them apart was going to be difficult for both of them.

That was one of the big things that Ashley had either failed to see or didn't care enough to acknowledge when making all these changes to accommodate her and Dave. She was going to separate the kids, and she didn't care. She was going to be responsible for breaking his heart but she went ahead and did it anyway.

On the first day of school, Marcy packed him an awesome lunch, and I actually booked the day off work so that I could take him. I could remember switching schools myself one time when I was a kid around the same grade, and it wasn't an easy thing to do. Josh had been through more of this kind of stuff in his young life than he should ever have been exposed to in ten lifetimes, and I felt bad for him.

Luckily, he was very resilient, and he always seemed to have a way of making lemonade when life had constantly given him lemons. And this was no exception. He went into this new school, with new kids, locked and loaded with a positive attitude, and it didn't take him long before he started to fit in. Things were definitely going alright in that avenue of his life, but in other areas things were not so good.

When I looked into his eyes, I could see the pain that he was struggling with—caused by the aftermath of what his mother had done by casting him aside in favour of her husband. It took a few months, I think, before he finally came to terms with what had happened. That's when the reality set in: the life he was now living with us was the only life he was going to have moving forward.

I don't believe that he ever truthfully accepted everything, nor do I believe he ever got past what that disconnect had done to him the day his mother said goodbye to him and walked away. It was a very sad thing to have to stand back and witness, and I honestly don't know if I'd be strong enough to watch another one of my kids be put into that position again and have to suffer through it.

He cried every single night at bedtime for weeks. Every. Single. Night.

And there was nothing I could do to take that pain away from him. I felt terrible and guilty and—in all honesty—I would have gladly taken his place if I could have so that he didn't have to endure it. Only time was going to heal those wounds, but even at that, there would be scars that were going to last a lifetime. Once he had moved in with us, travel between homes had become a bigger issue now than it had even been in the past.

We were still sending the kids via bus between our homes, and now that one of the kids resided with us, those travel arrangements would require modification yet again. What was going to have to happen now though was one kid or the other would be travelling weekly—so one weekend, I would send Josh to Ashley and the following weekend Ashley would send Edward to us. This would be the only way to maintain both parents seeing both kids every second weekend, and it also allowed the kids to see each other every weekend. What that meant though was that I was going to have to go that shady bus station *every* week now instead of every second week, and that was not something I was very excited about having to do.

The other downside to it was that it also meant that the kids would now be travelling by themselves instead of as a pair, and that travelling would be at an increased frequency which greatly increased the potential that one or the other might bear witness to some type of incident on one of the buses or in one of the bus stations.

If there was any other way I could have gotten the kids to where they had to go without using Greyhound, I would have taken it. After doing some research, though, my findings revealed that there was nothing else available that was affordable, so again there was no choice in the matter.

Twenty

A couple weeks after getting Josh settled into home and school, I had gone ahead and contacted Sylvia to start working on drawing up the papers to reflect the change in custody that had recently occurred. As with any court process, of course, it was going to take some time to get everything written up, forwarded to Ashley, signed off on, processed through the court, and finalized by the judge. Because I knew there was going to be a delay in all this, I had contacted the maintenance enforcement program to discuss a variance in my payment due the change in custody that had recently taken place.

Ashley had registered our agreement with the program shortly after she had moved the kids to Red Deer because, in an attempt to try and inconvenience her for moving them two hours away unannounced, I started mailing her child support cheque to her on the first of the month. Because it took a few days to arrive in Red Deer, and she couldn't use it in its entirety just to pay her rent, she decided to register it with the maintenance enforcement program so it would be directly deposited to her account on the first of every month.

This certainly had no negative impact on me. The maintenance enforcement program is only a burden to people who don't make their payments, and therefore it was no hindrance to me whatsoever. I actually found that it had some positive aspects to it.

Making payments through the program assured that there could be no question that I had indeed made my payments in full at the required intervals. Essentially it was one less thing that I had to worry about her claiming that I didn't do.

Upon engaging in conversation with the maintenance enforcement staff regarding the recent custody change, they were clear in communicating to me that policy stated that they were required to enforce the current court order in power until such time a judge made a variance to it. I explained to them that Ashley had recently turned full custody of Josh over to me, and therefore, I was no longer required to pay child support on both kids. They assured me there was nothing they could do unilaterally on their end.

However, if Ashley were to contact them and verify the information, there were some steps that could be taken to temporarily vary the child support order. They said, upon Ashley calling to confirm everything, she would then be required to write a letter stating the custody change that had taken place between us and then sign, date, and fax that letter in to them along with all the necessary identification to confirm she was in fact who she was claiming to be. At that point they could make a temporary variance to my support payments to reflect payment on only one kid instead of two until the new child support agreement had time to go through the court system again, be updated and make its way back to them.

So I called Ashley and informed her of what I was trying to get done, and that I would need her to submit the letter and all the other information the maintenance enforcement program would require from her on her end to proceed with my request. After contemplating my request for a few seconds, she flat out told me that she wasn't going to do it.

I couldn't believe it.

If anyone on this fucking planet knew full well the arrangement that had just been made with our kids, and the fact that one no longer resided under her care, it was her, but she still wasn't willing to sign off on it. She wanted to keep on receiving a full payment for two kids every month for as long as she could, and she was perfectly happy to rely on maintenance enforcement program to do it.

For three months I paid a child support payment to her based on two kids while also covering the running expenses of Josh. The month before the custody and child support order was scheduled for variance in court, I declined the upcoming payment to maintenance enforcement as it was being taken from me under false pretenses unbeknownst to them, and I had already overpaid in excess of a thousand dollars above what I was actually required to pay by law. These overpayments had started to affect my ability to provide for the people that lived in my household and I had enough with it.

Marcy was on maternity leave at that time and wasn't even bringing home fifty percent of her usual working income, so every dollar counted at that time. Within two or three days of that non-payment, the maintenance enforcement program had contacted my employer and requested that the funds required to cover the costs of the payment I had defaulted on be taken from my next payroll deposit and be sent to them.

I received a phone call from my employer shortly therefore to be notified of what maintenance enforcement had requested of them. I explained to my employer the situation that I had been put into with all the changes that had recently taken place with my kids and that I had in fact overpaid substantially at this point.

As we were now within a month of the scheduled court date anyways, I told my employers admin staff to go ahead and do whatever they had to in order to appease the maintenance enforcement program. As if all this wasn't ridiculous enough already, considering the circumstances, I had just filed my taxes for that year at the same time, and the six hundred dollar tax return I had coming back to me was instead intercepted on its way to my bank account and given to Ashley as well.

When the court date arrived, Sylvia made mention to the court that because of Ashley's dishonesty, I had been made to look non-credible to my employer. The court proceeded to vary the child support order to reflect the payment to Ashley for Edward and pro-rated that payment to start back when Josh had initially moved in with us nearly four months previous. As per my calculations, I had overpaid Ashley in child support now by nearly fourteen hundred dollars. Due to Ashley's role in all this, which was the only reason for any over payment to begin with, I was not required to make any more child support payments to her until the amounts had offset each other at which point my payments would resume as per the new agreement.

With all the court papers rewritten to encompass the changes that had recently taken place, I felt satisfied, for the time being anyways, that things were written up tight enough that Ashley wouldn't be able to take advantage of me any further.

Twenty-one

It was really nice to have Josh living under our roof at that point. Along with the fact that I now got to see him every day, I also knew he was no longer dealing with the stress of living with Dave. Most importantly I knew that he was safe, eating good meals, and wearing clothes that fit him. He had settled into his new school quite nicely, and the teachers began to compliment me almost immediately on how nice of a kid he was.

One thing that can be said about Josh, and something I am extremely proud of him for, is the fact that he is a well-mannered, genuinely nice guy. As time went on, Josh became more accustomed to the living arrangements he now had and eventually it just became the norm. Josh and Edward maintained their weekly travels between both homes, and Marcy and I plugged away at home in the basement.

Through hard work, long hours, and perseverance we had arrived at the finished point in our basement development. We let the kids pick the colours of their rooms and we had just recently finished the last of all the painting right as the carpet throughout had been installed. It looked amazing. It was a really awesome turn out. All that was left to do at that point was to install the baseboards and casings and upon the completion of that, it was ready to go.

The first thing we did was move Josh down to his new room which was much bigger than the one he had been using at the time and it wasn't located next to a screaming baby. That didn't quite go as well as I thought it would though.

After a few days, Josh started to get freaked out down there by himself and didn't want to sleep in his new room anymore. I could and I couldn't understand it at the same time. It was just a small basement, and the design had both bedrooms located right next to the stairs, so it wasn't like the rooms were isolated in a dark corner or something. Plus it was absolutely beautiful down there, everything was fresh and new, very comfortable.

But he was ten years old, and I get how kids' imaginations can grab hold of them sometimes, and this was clearly a textbook case of just that—he was down there by himself, it's understandable. So when we get up in the morning, we'd find him lying on the floor in the living room fast asleep. We never gave up though, we'd put him to bed down there every night and tell him, if he needed to come up, he could, no big deal.

At that time, we didn't have any extra furniture, so everything he had been using in the other bedroom when he was upstairs did, in fact, go down with him to his new room, which is why we'd find him lying on the floor. Luckily, he wouldn't be sleeping down there by himself for long.

It was the fall of 2010, and I found out that Ashley had yet again relocated to another place, only this time it was to a place called Sylvan Lake about twenty minutes from Red Deer where they had been living for the last few years

As an added twist to the whole story, I also learned it was actually just Ashley and Edward who had moved. I guess there must have been trouble in paradise—Ashley and Dave's relationship had crashed and burned and it was right around this time that their relationship officially ended. Less than two years after Ashley and Dave had conceived their second child, they were divorced and separated and when Ashley took Edward and moved away from Red Deer she left her two younger children behind.

Now Dave was in a similar type of predicament that I had been in since the day he had met me years earlier. He always had my mistakes to reflect on right from the go, and yet, here he was. Really what can be said for a guy who watched his girlfriend/wife try to screw her ex over time and time again any way possible and helped participate in it.

Karma is a real motherfucker.

It was only ever a matter of time with Ashley and Dave—that clock had been counting down right from the start. Who knows exactly what the reasons were that brought them together initially, but whatever those reasons were, they weren't strong enough to keep them together for very long. Dave never saw me, nor my kids ever again. As with so many others along the way, he was just another guy that came and went through Ashley's door. I think back to all the dumb things he had to say and how he preached to my family and me about how we needed to back off because he was the one raising my kids now, blah, blah, blah. More meaningless words have never been spoken by anyone.

Dave is nothing more than a memory, an irrelevant footnote to some particularly dumb chapters in my life and the lives of my two eldest boys.

My biggest concern at the time was that Edward had been forced to switch schools yet again. I once again reflected on my experience as a kid and the impact switching schools a single time had on me. What was the impact going to be on Edward who now had been in and out of five or six schools over the last two or three years?

I knew that classrooms from one school to another would, of course, be learning different material at different speeds and that alone meant the constant school moves were going to be detrimental. Unfortunately, I was still helpless in all this, and without thousands of dollars to spend on a lawyer to try to take control of a situation that was clearly poisonous to my kid, there wasn't anything else I could do.

Turns out, all I had to do was wait, and things would come full circle.

Within a couple months of Ashley and Edward moving into their new place, Ashley informed me that they were now planning on moving back to Edmonton. After all that time that they had been gone—Ashley claiming she had moved my kids away because they had a better life awaiting them in Red Deer—they were now coming back to where they had started, and everything she had done to the kids throughout that process had been for nothing.

The insane amount of driving Marcy and I were subjected to in order to get the kids, that was for nothing. Sending the kids back and forth on sketchy Greyhounds a year and a half, that was all for nothing. The kids being moved six ways to Sunday over those years and the multiple school changes that undoubtedly crippled their ability to keep on top of their schoolwork, ultimately putting them behind in their studies, that was all for nothing.

It was all for nothing. For nothing! I just can't stress that enough. There wasn't a single positive thing that came out of Ashley moving to Red Deer to start a new life as she claimed at the time. Not a single thing. And now here she was moving back without so much as a pot to piss in. She may as well never even have left in the first place—she would have been better off.

The fact she was planning yet another move, one which would mean a second school change in the first three months of that school year, had me very concerned. How could I possibly let this happen to Edward? I asked Ashley where in Edmonton the apartment she'd lined up was, and she admitted she didn't have one lined up, and that she and Edward would be couch surfing for the next little while until she could figure out what she was going to do.

I couldn't believe what I was hearing. I seriously thought she was kidding when she said that.

At that point I knew I had no choice in the matter any longer, I had to intervene and take control of the situation. I told her that couch surfing wasn't going to be an acceptable arrangement for a child, and that I wasn't going to allow it. I pleaded with her to let Edward go and let him come live with us at our house. Marcy and I had the infrastructure within our home to accommodate him with his own room, good meals, plus his brother and his half-brother were there as was the stability he needed so badly in his life.

Ashley wouldn't agree to it. She just would not let him go.

Eventually, as move day got closer and closer, it came to the point where I decided if she didn't voluntarily release Edward to me before they moved, that I was going to take her to court and have him removed from her custody. Considering the circumstances in her life that she had created not only for herself, but for Edward as well, it was obvious that she couldn't look after him properly, and this was something she had to think about very carefully. It was clear for his success and well-being he needed to get out from under her wing.

Eventually she decided that she would let him go and let him come live with us. I really wasn't expecting that. I thought for sure it would be a cold day in hell before she would ever turn the reins of Edward over to me. If nothing else, I was expecting that at bare minimum it was likely going to result in another court date.

When Ashley said that I could take custody of Edward, I felt a huge weight lifted off my shoulders. Marcy and I would now have custody of both of the kids for the first time ever, and for the first time in several years, I would no longer have to worry about either one of them and whether or not their basic needs amongst other things were being met because, under our roof, that wasn't going to be an issue.

This was a repeat, for Marcy and me, in terms of the responsibilities and preparation we had to make for Josh's arrival in the previous year right around the same time. Edward was set to move in to our house in just a little under two weeks, so for the next week or so, Marcy and I were busy at the school getting him registered, paying his school fees, and getting his school supplies in order. I had anticipated that, when Edward did move in with us, the situation with him was likely going be a bit more complicated and difficult than it had been with Josh. Not only had he had spent an additional year with Ashley by this time, but he was also much closer to her than Josh had ever been. I could never have possibly imagined, though, just how difficult things were going to become over time.

Due to the issues that we had with Ashley, financially, when Josh had come to live with us in the previous year, I made it clear to Ashley that, this time, before I would even load one suitcase into my vehicle the day I was scheduled to pick Edward up, that I would first require a signed and dated letter from her. That letter would need to be written to include all the information child maintenance would require to be able to temporarily vary the child support agreement currently in place until the court could make the permanent changes.

In this case, it was to state that she no longer had custody of either of our kids, and therefore, no payment would be required to be made to her following the day I picked him up. I knew Ashley's only true concern in all this was that she may now be required to pay child support to me for the kids, which was something she had made clear to me in the past that she would never do.

As a matter of fact, she was so against paying me anything for child support that she would've backed out of the custody agreement we had just made simply to prevent that from happening, regardless of whether she compromised Edward's future in the process or not. So after some thought, and in the best interest of Edward and getting him the hell out of there, I offered her a deal to put her mind at ease over it. I told her once she got back on her feet, as long as she contributed to the expenses of the children in whatever capacity she could, I would never pursue her for child support. Whatever she could swing, be it section seven expenses, school fees, whatever, I would take that as a genuine effort towards her trying to contribute, and that was good enough for me.

Marcy and I both had decent jobs, and we could look after the rest. She agreed to my offer and said she would write the letter I had requested and provide me with it the day I picked Edward up. When moving day did arrive, Ashley no longer had a vehicle, so I ended up having to drive all the way to where they were residing in Sylvan Lake to pick up Edward and all his belongings. I knew this would be the last time I would ever have to make that trek, so I just did it. When I arrived at the place they had been living at the preceding months, it was a one-bedroom apartment where Edward had been sleeping in the living room. It certainly wasn't a place that suited the needs of one adult and one child living there full-time—and certainly not what one could call a cozy place to live.

To my disbelief, Ashley asked me if she could thumb a ride back to Edmonton with us that day. She never had any intention of pitching any money in for gas, of course, but that didn't stop her from asking anyways. I wanted to tell her to fuck right off, but when I looked at her that day, though, she was—for lack of better words—pathetic. Absolutely pathetic. I actually felt sorry for her because everything in her life had gone so ridiculously wrong even though she was the only one to blame for why it had.

This was nothing more than karma coming back full circle, and it was late getting to that party. I was so relieved to know that I would no longer have to put my children at risk by sending them on Greyhounds that I couldn't express it enough, and I guess that's why I ended up giving her the ride she so desperately needed that day—even though I could hardly stand to look at her.

We loaded up all the possessions that Edward was bringing with him along with whatever shit of hers that would fit on top of that, and off we went. This was a move done in typical fashion for Ashley, and I'm sure this is how it all went down the many time's she's moved over the years. When we walked out of that apartment that day, she didn't clean a single thing, she left all the lights and the TV on. Any furniture and other belongings that couldn't fit in my vehicle were left behind, and when Ashley closed the sliding balcony door behind her that day, it was now somebody else's problem.

Twenty-two

The two-hour drive back home that day, for me, was awkward, and I really couldn't wait for it to be over. I even ended up having to go out of my way to drive her to where she was planning on staying—a friend's place in the interim until she could figure things out.

When Edward and I finally arrived home, it was official: all my kids were now under our roof, and I no longer had to worry about the well-being of any of them, and that felt awesome. Sadly, receiving full custody of Edward would prove to be a daunting task that took its toll on me and the other members of the household, and eventually even on my marriage for a brief period as well.

I'm not saying he was a bad kid, but he was stubborn as a fucking mule and, just like Josh, never had any intention of leaving his mother to come and live at our house. Furthermore, he had full intentions of driving that fact home to us the entire time he lived under our roof. As I had with Josh when he had come to live with us the previous year, I felt empathy for Edward as well because, including the new school that we had enrolled him in, this would be his third school in just the first three months of that year.

His initial school prior to Ashley and Dave splitting, his school briefly in Sylvan Lake, and now, moving in with us, he was switching schools again. I wish I could say that, like Josh, Edward was going to graduate with the kids he met the day he started school in our community, but that wasn't going to be the case with him unfortunately.

In the interim, I had once again contacted Sylvia to begin the process of writing up the paperwork to finalize us taking custody of Edward. When we sat down to discuss the details of the agreement, Sylvia asked about child support. I explained to her what I had agreed to with Ashley as far as no support required so long as she help out whenever possible. Sylvia felt that what we needed to do *instead* was to put the child support "in reserve".

Essentially what that meant was this: there wouldn't be a monthly child support payment assigned to Ashley so long as she maintained the agreement we had made between us. In other words, so long as she played ball, it could stay in reserve. However, should she choose not to hold up her end of the deal to the best of her ability, and I felt I needed to pursue her for financial support to help with the kids, it was an easy item to revisit in court. If it wasn't placed in reserve, it would be difficult to undo the "no-payment clause" in the agreement and have child support reinstated at a later date.

I was still walking on eggshells with Ashley at this point, and I wasn't sure how that reserve clause was going to affect our arrangement. I was worried she may refuse it and pull the pin to prevent any binding circumstances being placed on her now or sometime in the future. So I met with Ashley and gave her the paperwork regarding the change of custody. She did of course inquire about the reserve child support clause, and I explained to her exactly what it meant, and reiterated to her again that if she did the best she could to help out with the kids whenever she could, it wasn't something that would ever need to be revisited.

To my surprise, she did sign off on the agreement, and from there she returned the paperwork to Sylvia who—as quickly as can be—ran it through the court system, finalizing everything.

And so, we all lived happily ever after.

The end.

Or not. I wish that I could say that was all there is to this story, but it isn't.

I had taken note over the previous couple years that Edward seemed like he was starting to withdraw a bit. He was becoming more and more introverted, and conversations with him were becoming shorter, very one-sided as he didn't have much to say. It was becoming hard to get him to engage in conversation.

Naturally, I was worried about it, so I ended up taking him in to the doctor where he was given a referral for counselling. As luck would have it, the counsellor was located right there in Morinville, and we were able to see him outside of our normal hours of work so we didn't have to use a large portion of our vacation days to attend our appointments. His name was Warren and he specialized in working with kids just like Edward.

The timing on the counselling was ideal, for Edward was really starting to become difficult in pretty much every aspect of his life. At ten years old, he had to fight and argue with me over absolutely everything. Whether it was homework or having a shower, chores, whatever it might be, it was a fight, and I was getting really tired of it. He was becoming extremely difficult to live with. He wanted to go back and live with his mom, and I think that he felt if he got under my skin deep enough that I'd send him back to her—but because I cared about him and his future, I had no intention of ever sending him away.

I knew if he was to have any chance of success in life it would be under the wing of Marcy and I and not Ashley's. She was the number one reason everything had gotten so messed up to begin with, and yet both of my kids' loyalties remained with her. This is where Warren shed some light on what was actually happening here.

He explained to us how studies have shown that children will always step on the people in their lives who they know will never abandon them under any circumstances. Conversely, they will always tread lightly around the ones that they know will, and that was exactly what was happening in my case. That was a lightbulb moment for me. Previously, I couldn't fathom why things were the way they were, but now it all made sense, and the kids were very much correct in their assumption that it wouldn't have taken much for Ashley to just walk away from them. After all, she had already walked away and abandoned her other two kids.

Over the course of the next couple months, many interesting things came out of the counselling we were undergoing. Warren was amazing. He had answers to everything we were going though day-to-day with Edward and what we could do to counteract the less than desirable behaviours from him. He would even occasionally spend some time with Marcy and I as well to ensure that our marriage wasn't suffering in all this. He wanted to make sure that we too had positive avenues that we could utilize should the added Edward-related stress start to impact our marriage in a negative way.

I think it was safe to say we were slowly starting to make progress with Edward when word came down that the arrangement we had with Warren was going to be changing. The government was planning to close down the office in Morinville, and Warren had decided to start his own practice in the light of the news. This meant we would no longer have access to him unless we paid out of pocket, which we didn't have the money to do. We decided, in the interim, we would have to put the counselling on the back burner and see what kind of results we could yield with the skillset Warren had already equipped us with.

Twenty-three

School was another major issue we were facing with Edward at the time. He refused to do any homework or put any effort into his studies whatsoever. Even with me coaching him at home, he didn't care. I knew by the end of this first school year he would be even further behind and that the process would continue to snowball until there was no hope that he could ever catch up.

Near the completion of the school year, I inquired as to whether the school felt there would be any value in Edward possibly repeating a grade in an attempt to give him a chance to catch up with everything he was struggling with. I was informed at that time that schools today no longer make kids repeat grades because it had been shown that it's too hard on their self-esteem. Even if they are so far behind they can't make heads or tails out of what they are learning, the school will push them through anyways. I must admit I couldn't understand how that could be an effective solution, but I'm also not a specialist in child learning and development.

Thinking back to when I was a kid, the thought of failing and having to possibly repeat another grade alone was typically motivation enough to make me pull my socks up and put the extra effort in. Had the possibility of failure not existed when I was in school, I likely wouldn't have cared what my marks were either, and my efforts in school would have been even less than what they were.

I could certainly relate to how Edward may have felt being in a position where he was behind everybody else on the learning curve. I had actually been sent back to school myself that year to acquire another level of certification that my employer required me to have. I had completed my post-secondary training about ten years prior, and on my first day back to school, it was evident that I was very much behind the eight ball on the learning curve compared to the students who had been in school the previous year and were simply continuing from where they had left off. It made me feel like I was stupid. It made me frustrated and angry, and it made me want to quit and go home. That's how I felt being behind everybody else on the learning scale, and I'm sure that was exactly how Edward was feeling—and he was only ten. Having said that, if he did feel that way, he was handling it much better than I did under the same circumstances.

You would think that, seeing as Ashely's other two kids were now two hours away and her involvement with them was minimal—if it existed at all—and she had no other responsibilities whatsoever tying her down, she would have wanted to spend as much time as she could with Josh and Edward and perhaps lend a helping hand with the school and the behavioral issues, but that was not the case. She would only spend four days a month with the kids, and with the massive amount of dating she had now once again become involved in, she had no intention of committing any more of her time to them than that.

On top of that, to demonstrate just how little she clearly cared about the kids, she hadn't contributed a single dime to help cover any of the living expenses or section seven expenses that she'd agreed she would help us out with. I came to the conclusion it was pointless to dwell on the facts in all this, if nothing else, that simply would have driven me crazy and at that time my energy needed to be focused in other areas of my life.

One such area revolved around a decision Marcy and I had just recently made to purchase a bigger house. The house we were living in at the time did do the job, but it was pretty tight considering there were five of us living there and we were tired of everybody crawling over top of each other. By this time, my credit had been fully re-established and between that and the equity we now had in our current house, we were cleared by the bank to go ahead and purchase a different home if we wanted. And this time we could do so without the help of a co-signer.

Marcy and I both had fond memories of the acreage by Josephburg, and so we set our sights on trying to find something along those lines. We still weren't crazy about the general area of where we were living, and although we now had the option to move anywhere that we wanted to, including back to Fort Saskatchewan, we couldn't bring ourselves to make Josh and Edward change schools yet again simply because we wanted to relocate. That is exactly what had happened to them time and time again living with Ashley. Marcy and I simply refused to perpetuate that vicious cycle.

We decided we would stick close to Morinville so the kids could maintain their current schools and not be uprooted yet again. The move back to Fort Saskatchewan where Marcy and I really wanted to be would have to wait until later on in life. As it turned out, when we did go searching for acreages, we couldn't find anything even close to our price point. It was unobtainable for us. Most were older homes anyways—well-kept, of course, with mature tree canopies and shelter belts, but just not exactly what we had envisioned in our minds. After crunching some numbers, we determined we could build a new house and pretty much create exactly what we wanted within the budget that we had.

It wasn't going to be a high-end home by any means, but it would serve our family much better than the house that we were living in at the time. Unfortunately, this endeavour would prove to be quite a shit show as well, and if we'd have known that in advance, it's hard to say what we would have done. As the old saying goes, hindsight is always twenty–twenty. Having chosen the path we wanted to venture down together, we began our search for a piece of land, and after some searching, we came across a piece that was perfect for what we needed, so we made an offer on it and listed our house for sale on the market at the same time.

Everything in this deal hinged on everything else, and that made planning anything in advance very difficult for us. The bank wouldn't give us money for a piece of raw land, so we had to buy the land outright before we could secure the financing to build the house. Therefore, we would need to sell the house we were living in first so we could use the equity from that sale to purchase the land and get things rolling with the bank. In turn, that then meant we would have to try to find a place to rent once our house was sold until our new house was built and ready to be occupied—something that typically takes about a year or so.

Living in a small town like Morinville, there weren't a lot of places available to rent to begin with, and without knowing when our house would sell exactly, and what date we'd need to vacate by, we very well couldn't commit to renting a place without that information. This meant we would have to wait until the place was confirmed sold and then quickly go try to find somewhere to rent.

Seeing as Marcy and I have always tried to be proactive with decisions in our life together, it would prove unnerving for us to have to leave everything until the last minute. As it turned out, our house wasn't on the market for very long before we had some people who were interested. They made us an offer, we accepted, and the deal was written and sealed.

At that point we had six weeks to vacate the house, and we still hadn't lined up a place to go. Now that we knew all this was going to go ahead, Marcy wasted no time in starting the search for a rental for us. As it turned out, she could only find one place in the entire town that was for rent, and even that had literally just become available a couple of days previous, so we had no choice but to take it. It was in a four-suite condo building, and the unit that we would be renting had two levels that were each about seven hundred square feet—and it had three bedrooms.

It was extremely tiny and less than ideal for the five of us that were going to be living there for the next year or so, but it would have to suffice. In the meantime, Marcy and I began the tedious process of packing, cleaning, and starting to make the first of two moves in the next year or so. In this first move, because the place we were moving into was so small, we shifted the majority of our stuff into a storage facility, and only planned to take what we absolutely needed with us. It wasn't long before we were down to just the bare essentials left at our house—we'd be able to quickly move that over to the rental house when the time came.

While all this was going on, Edward was continuing to struggle academically, so after a couple meetings with the school, they put a request in to a learning and development clinic to assist with the issues we were having. This would prove to be a bit of a commitment on my part because the clinic was located about forty-five minutes away in downtown Edmonton, and any of the appointments that we had would require me to take a day off work to get him there.

Luckily for me, my employer was a very family-first type of organization, and so getting time off for stuff like that wasn't a big deal. I would just have to utilize some of my vacation days to get him in for his appointments, which I had no issue in doing whatsoever. So I went ahead and booked our first appointment with the learning and development clinic, and a couple weeks later, when the day arrived... we didn't end up making it there because of an issue that had occurred that morning.

Twenty-four

Before I tell you what happened, I would like say that if there was any way that I could go back in time and change the way I handled things that day, I would do it in a heartbeat. Even now, all these years later, I wish that day never happened. The blowout that occurred that morning was undoubtedly the direct result of all the issues between Edward and I that had been building up, and when the events of that morning unfolded, it pushed me passed my breaking point, and I was in the wrong.

Here's what happened.

I'd taken the day off work and Edward was off school so we could attend the appointment at the learning and development clinic. There was a kids' science experiment kit that had made its way into our house from somewhere, and Edward happened to be playing around with it. That morning before Marcy left for work, as she walked past Edward in the kitchen, she instructed him not to play around with it, and that they could sit down that evening and do a couple experiments if he wanted.

With that, Marcy took off to drop Michael off at daycare and go to work, and Josh set off to school. I ran downstairs to use the computer before Edward and I had to go. We didn't have much time, so I just left him upstairs while I went down. I remember hearing a loud "pop" type noise come from upstairs, but I quickly dismissed it as I was busy trying to wrap up what I was doing on the computer before we had to hit the road.

Within thirty seconds Edward came running downstairs, panicked and upset. When I went upstairs, I was horrified at what I saw. He had created a concoction of some sort in a bottle with some chemicals that were included in that science kit. He'd added a red dye to the mixture as well, and when the chemicals had been combined with each other they began to expand from their original size many times over. When it had started to spill out from the top of the bottle and all over the table and the floor he'd panicked.

And closed the lid on the bottle.

What happened next was incredible. The pressure building up inside the bottle blew the top off with such force that it sprayed up as high as the ceiling and the dye that was present in the mixture stained anything it came into contact with including the ceiling, the walls, the curtains, literally anything within a fifteen-foot radius.

I ended up coming unglued on Edward. This was in no way, shape, or form a healthy or constructive way for me to deal with what had just happened, and when I did lose my temper, I ended up saying a bunch of shit to him that I just didn't mean. As the adult in this situation—and not just the adult but the *parent* for that matter—I shouldn't have met him with rage the way that I did that day. I simply could have placed a stiff punishment on him and drawn it out over a lengthy period of time to assure he got the message loud and clear and that would have been sufficient.

I mean, the damage was already done, and there was absolutely nothing to be gained by blowing a gasket and scarring the kid in the process. If only I had a little more clarity in the moment when this all went down. I knew this wasn't some intentional act of sabotage, and even though he had been warned not to mess around with what had essentially been the cause of all this, he was just a kid messing around, and it blew up on him (literally as well as figuratively).

I called Marcy and told her what had just happened, and that I needed her to come home as soon as possible. When she walked through the door and into the kitchen to assess the damage, she was speechless. Upon word spreading to Carol as to what had happened and in order to best diffuse the situation at our house, she came to grab Edward and take possession of him for a day or so until things had cooled off a bit at home.

To this day, I feel regret and sorrow towards Edward over the way I handled the events of that morning, and although I did apologize to him for my awful behaviour and lack of judgment in light of the events that did occur, it was too little, too late. Some things you can just never go back on, and for me, this is one of those things.

Because this house wasn't even technically ours anymore, and the people who had bought it from us were now within weeks of their possession day, Marcy and I had a major problem on our hands, one that certainly wasn't going to go away on its own. The first thing we started with was the clean-up. It took hours of cleaning with both of us working at it just to get the walls cleaned up, the baseboards, the windows, the cabinets, and everywhere else that had been spattered with the pink solution. Sadly, even after all that cleaning, it was still possible to see the pink spray pattern that had imprinted itself on the walls upon impact.

At one point, we were actually thinking that we may have to repaint the room in order to correct the problem. We ended up getting lucky with the walls and were able to completely erase the dye marks, but unfortunately that wasn't going be the case with the ceiling. The majority of the pink splatter that was ejected from the bottle that day had impacted the ceiling which was textured with stipple, and that had soaked up the dye like a sponge. There would be no easy fix to this problem. It was going to have to be painted.

The only workable solution we could come up with was applying a stain-blocking primer to the affected area and repainting. By the time all the cleaning was done and the painting had been completed, we had invested many hours of labour and hundreds of dollars in material. We didn't have a choice, it had to be fixed. After all the hard work, money spent, and stress, we got it as close to perfect as it was ever going to get. I could still very much see areas in that ceiling that had a pinkish tinge to them, but that was probably only because I knew what had happened in that room and knew where to look.

The place actually looked better than it did before we had started—and just in time to give it away to somebody else. We immediately moved ourselves and the rest of our stuff out of the house and into our new location before any other disasters could occur, and when possession day did arrive for the people who bought the house, I never heard anything derogatory from the move-in inspection, so I guess Marcy and I had done an acceptable job.

This initial relocation that we made would mark the beginning of some of the busiest, craziest, and most stressful times that Marcy and I would ever experience together.

Twenty-five

So we moved into the rental, and just as we had expected, it was really tight with all five of us. As with every other place we had ever lived since we had all three kids under one roof, we had the traditional and reoccurring problem it seemed of not having enough bedrooms to go around. And here we were once again one bedroom short. In the experiences Marcy and I have had over the years with finding a place to live for our family, it has always been really hard to find something that will house a family of five. A family of four is no problem, but five, good luck.

Seeing as this was a three-bedroom unit, we decided we would give Josh and Edward their own rooms, and Marcy and I would share a room with Michael. Our room was barely big enough for our bed, so we really had no choice but set up a little spot for him on the floor to sleep. I felt bad about him having to sleep down there, and so after a couple days, I opted to take the floor instead for the duration of our stay so that he didn't have to.

Josh and Edward were gone to Ashley's every second weekend anyway, so during those weekends when their rooms were unoccupied, we would put Michael to bed in one of those rooms and I would get a couple days in my own bed and off of the floor to give my back a rest.

It was during this time I received what I considered to be a very disturbing phone call while I was at work one day. It was a call from child protective services. The woman on the other end of the line had called me to talk about the person Ashley was currently in a relationship with and had been for the past couple months.

She couldn't stress enough to me that this person was unfit to be around children. Those were her exact words. She actually referred to this guy as vile and stated boldly to me (and I quote) "he doesn't need to be around your children." She wouldn't elaborate on any details, but she warned me time and again during that phone call to keep my kids away from this person even if that meant refusing access of the kids to Ashley.

I was sick to my stomach hearing all of this as Josh and Edward had already spent a few weekends in this guy's presence while visiting Ashley. As a matter of fact, maybe a week or two prior to that call from child protective services, Ashley had texted me telling me that she and this guy had made plans to build a house together and that they wanted a fifty–fifty split custody of the kids upon completion of it.

I contacted Ashley immediately after that phone call and she flat out said everything I had been told was bullshit. She denied everything and said it was nothing more than slander and that this person she was seeing was a good guy and I had no reason to worry. According to Ashley this guy had a court case underway to clear his name of this "slander" he had been falsely accused of, and everyone, including me, would see his innocence in all this when he won that court case.

This type of behaviour was completely typical of Ashley. Nearly every guy she had ever dated was, in her mind, the guy she was now going to get married to, and live with forever. For me, what it came down to was a complete stranger's word as to his own character against child protective services—who had contacted me out genuine concern for the safety of my children, trying to prevent something inconceivable from possibly happening to them.

Armed with that information, I knew I certainly wasn't willing to allow the possibility of something detrimental occurring either. However, Ashley disregarded anything she heard that negatively impacted her boyfriend's reputation even though she literally had only known him for a couple of months at that time. She fully embraced everything he had to say and went as far as the act of defending him even though she very well may have been endangering Josh and Edward by doing so.

At that point, I had no choice but to refuse her any access to the children until she made arrangements where she could see the kids without her boyfriend being around them. Luckily for me this standoff didn't last long. As with so many other guys along the way, it wasn't long before Ashely and this guy split up, and her ridiculous dreams of a life with him evaporated. At that point, he exited the picture permanently, and I let out a sigh of relief.

Back on the home front, now that Marcy and I had secured the land we were going to build our house on, we were busy selecting the builder we were going to use, working on the floorplan, and trying to get the utility companies lined up to service the property. We had lots of appointments with different builders at that point, and after visiting several, we made the decision as to which one we wanted to use.

After finalizing the floorplan, we had made an appointment to go in and give the builder a deposit, but things kind of went south at the last minute. It's kind of a shame because Marcy and I had already invested a bunch of time into picking colours, flooring, and cabinets, and it was all for nothing. Because I'm a plumber, I wanted to do the install of the plumbing system myself, and although doing something like that undoubtedly takes dollars and cents right out of the builder's pocket, they agreed they would allow me to do so.

Their proposal was that they would give us a credit on our bill for the amount their contractor had quoted them to do the install, but when they presented us with the amount of money that they were willing to credit back as per their contractor, I knew it was bullshit. It was about thirty percent of what it actually should have been. I argued with that builder about it for about ten minutes before I ripped up the cheque and walked out the door.

It didn't take us long to find another company that was more than willing to build the house for us, and following some reference verifications, we wasted no time in cutting them a cheque to get the process underway. During this time, we were also in talks with the utility companies regarding the servicing of our land. We needed power and natural gas brought to the site, and although there were other farms and acreages in the area, this was going to turn into a way bigger clusterfuck than anybody could ever have imagined.

If it had been possible to get the utility companies to more closely assess the installations prior to us buying the land, it likely would have changed everything regarding the decisions Marcy and I had made going into this. Naturally, no revenue generating organization is going to spend too much time, effort, manpower or resources to dig into something that may not even go ahead, so when dealing with utility companies pre-contract for services, it's a generic process in which you don't necessarily get a detailed investigation of what the installation might involve.

Initially, the word came in from the gas company that there was a high-pressure line directly across the road that they could tap into and drag over to our property. They said it wasn't a huge deal and this would fall under the standard six-thousand-dollar new service installation fee. Upon touching base with the power company, they were certain that they would be able to utilize the high voltage power poles installed down the entire length of our road to run a low voltage line from the neighbour down the road to our property poles.

They told us essentially the same thing, namely, that a seven-thousand-dollar bill would bring power to our property. Those numbers were reasonable and within the ballpark of what we were expecting, so we were thinking we were good to go. Such would not be the case. These certainly started out as exciting times, but unfortunately that excitement was going to be short lived.

Twenty-six

During the time all this other stuff was going on with our build, I had gone ahead and rebooked the appointment Edward and I had previously missed with the learning and development clinic to address the issues he was experiencing. I felt it was way more important now than ever before considering the blowout that had recently taken place, that he had to get in there and receive the help he needed to address all the issues he may have been dealing with at that time.

I knew the learning and development clinic would be a wealth of resources for him and could offer him many different options. They could sense the urgency of the situation and were quick in getting us booked in again. When the appointment arrived this time around, I made damn sure we were there. The doctor ran his tests and had a bunch of both written and verbal questions for Edward to answer.

After a few hours of diagnosis—as had been the findings of the other doctors in the past—he too was convinced Edward was suffering from ADHD. Even though Ashley had both Josh and Edward on meds nearly the entire time they had resided with her for the treatment of ADHD, I had stopped administering those pills to them once they we under my care because I wasn't convinced the diagnosis was correct.

Nevertheless, I took the doctor at his word because he was the specialist, and I agreed to start Edward on medication once again. He prescribed us a particular brand that he speculated would best suit the particular ADHD symptoms that Edward was suffering from, rebooked us in a month's time for follow up, and sent us on our way. That first medication he prescribed had some really odd side effects for Edward, and within two days of being on those pills, he couldn't fall asleep for his life.

He'd lay there awake for hours on end, and so I pulled the pin and stopped administering those pills to him. We went back and got another prescription for a different type of medication, and when he was on those meds, he couldn't stay awake, he was drowsy all the time. Eventually, we found one that didn't seem to offer any side effects, but it also didn't seem to do jack shit for any of the issues he was having either. They were mega-expensive and seemed like a complete waste of time, but we carried on using them in hope that it may eventually yield some results.

What I found, though, was the same results I had observed in the past with all this, no change in behaviour, no change in school performance, no change in anything whatsoever. I'm not saying ADHD isn't a real disorder, or that the medications made for it don't work, I'm just saying that, in Edward's case, and Josh's too for that matter when he was on similar meds, I never saw any demonstrable results whatsoever. In my mind, it must have either been an incorrect diagnosis, or the meds were just ineffective and didn't work on my kids.

Truth was, Edward was getting more and more distant and introverted, and I wasn't so sure I was ever going get him back from where he was headed. On top of that, I was starting to get a lot of phone calls from the school for numerous things regarding his behaviour. I have always taken any concerns from the school regarding my children very seriously, but during these times, I was starting to feel that the school was being a little excessive as to what they felt warranted a phone call to me while I was at work.

I honestly think the vice principal just had enough of Edward and was simply tired of all the little piddly stuff that was occurring daily, and he was at the end of his rope. There weren't any serious behavioral issues happening here, but that VP would call me almost every single day. He would report to me about how Edward had been wearing his hood in the hallway, which wasn't allowed, or that he had worn his hat into a classroom, stuff like that. I get that there are rules, and I also get that Edward wasn't following those rules as he should have been, but the principal calling me at work to discuss every little thing was starting to get a bit ridiculous. I felt this was something that the school and Edward could work out between themselves through whatever means necessary be it detention or otherwise.

I tried talking to Edward about the many facets in his life that had me concerned, and that did absolutely nothing, so I decided likely the best thing I could do was to make a plan to enrol him in counselling again in the near future. In the meantime, Marcy and I decided that some sports might be a good way to help him build some self-esteem and possibly help him crawl out of his shell, so we decided to enrol both Josh and Edward in soccer. I asked Ashley if she could pay the soccer fees for one of the kids, and of course, she claimed she had no money.

By this point, Marcy and I had both the kids under our full-time care for over two years, and Ashley hadn't given us a single penny to help with anything. Not one single penny. Any time I asked for monetary contributions from her, she would just blow it off like it wasn't her problem. That certainly wasn't part of the original deal we had made when I agreed to take both kids, and it was starting to piss me off. Marcy and I ended up paying the soccer fees for both of them and enrolled them anyways.

Because we lived in a rural community, it meant that games were going to be scattered all over the place, and some could be as far as an hour away from home. This was another shining example of how lousy of a parent Ashley truly is. The kids would naturally want her to watch them at their games, but she would only drive as far as Morinville, and that was it. If the games were any further away than that, she just couldn't be bothered, and she wouldn't attend.

I used to feel bad for the kids when she wouldn't come, but truthfully, that was probably better anyways, because anytime she would show up, she would typically bring a couple people out with her, and they would sit there on the sidelines smoking cigarettes. Between her and whomever she brought out with her, there was a cigarette burning at all times it seemed, and it was embarrassing as hell. I could tell the parents and other bystanders trying to enjoy the game were annoyed as the cigarette smoke from Ashley and her acquaintances wafted through the crowd and occasionally even into the group of kids that were playing soccer in the field.

I felt bad for the kids as they would always flock to Ashley during breaks or at the end of the game, and I knew they were being judged right alongside of her by everybody in attendance. I used to tell myself at that time that things could really be much worse and that Ashley's minimal involvement with the kids was actually a blessing in disguise. Both the kids could still have been living with her, and that would only have created a much worse situation.

As if things for Marcy and I weren't already action packed and financially draining enough, word came down that Josh was going to need braces. This was going to be a big expense. Over eight thousand dollars to be exact. Between Marcy and I, we had about four thousand dollars available to us that we could utilize through our benefit packages at work, but there will still going to be around four thousand dollars that wasn't covered.

This was a big-ticket item, of course, and it was a much higher priority item than most of the other things that kids require from a monetary standpoint throughout the process of growing up. I knew if we didn't invest the money to get his teeth fixed, there was a strong possibility it could be one of those lifelong things that could be a hindrance to his confidence and self-esteem when it came to different avenues in his life.

Marcy and I were already strapped for cash as it was, what with all the expenses we currently had at that time, and with no help financially from Ashley, trying to pay for something like braces would prove very difficult for us to do. I approached Ashley and asked her if she would be willing to make the monthly payments on the uncovered portion of the braces if we were to go ahead and get them. I expressed my concerns to her about how not getting his teeth fixed more than likely was going to have a negative impact on him well into his future and that braces would be nothing more than an investment that kept paying itself back over and over again.

She agreed that it was something that needed to be done, and she also agreed she would make the monthly payment on the balance left owing after getting the braces put on. That was good enough for me. That little bit of help was all that I ever expected from her to begin with, and I remember thinking to myself that it was about damn time she paid some of the expenses related to her kids. So we went ahead and had the procedure done.

The payments on the balance owing worked out to be about two hundred dollars a month based over twenty months. When the first payment came due, I asked Ashley for the money, and she paid it. As a matter of fact, she made the first four payments totalling about eight hundred dollars before she decided she was done with it.

Those were the only payments that she would ever make, and that was the only money that she would ever give to me towards the kids. Ever. As for the remaining payments, Marcy and I ended up having to make them. Ashley outright told me that she refused to give me money for anything and that included for any expenses related to our children. She felt she should be exempt in paying anything for the kids and that it should fall solely on my shoulders to provide for them.

I decided right then and there that I had enough of her bullshit. And as soon as the new house was finished and we were moved in, I was taking her to court for child support and making her officially responsible to contribute to the kids by doing so. Ashley had really screwed us again, and because monthly payments to an orthodontist wasn't something Marcy and I had planned on having to make, my visa was about to take a big old shit kicking.

Twenty-seven

This wasn't the only negative financial news we were facing at that time either—all the bad news regarding the house we were building had mounted and was starting to unfold at that time as well. It began initially with the power company who had come back to us with less than desirable news. They had approached the power company who had ownership of all the high voltage wiring and power poles that ran passed the front of our acreage and asked them if they could utilize those power poles to run the low voltage wiring that would be servicing our house.

They were told if they wanted to use the existing poles, they would have to pay an annual fee to that company indefinitely. Naturally this wasn't something our electricity provider was willing to do and sign off on, so it was up in the air as to what might be happening with it. Marcy and I couldn't quite understand what the issue was because there was a farm with an old house on it located a half-mile away and the power service was brought to that location utilizing those same poles.

Apparently, the days of being realistic about things were gone, and the big priority of this other power company was now rooted in trying to grab a few extra dollars for the foreseeable future from the little guy, which in this case was Marcy and me. After some research, I found out that this other power company was in fact a billion-dollar giant, and through their course of action in trying to make a couple extra dollars off something that would never have costed them a single penny to begin with, they had essentially contributed to helping temporarily cripple Marcy and me financially.

At the end of all the negotiations between the two power companies and their inability to come to any type of agreement, it was decided the electrical service to our property had to be run underground from over a kilometer away at a cost of over forty thousand dollars, and Marcy and I were on the hook to pay half of that. As I mentioned earlier during the planning stages of our house, we had budgeted seven thousand dollars for the electrical service, and because of this nonsense we were now on the hook to pay twenty-two thousand for it.

Furthermore, within a week or two of receiving that news, Marcy called me at work one day, upset and crying. We had just received a letter from the gas company, and as it turned out, there had been a mistake in the initial quote as to the cost of splicing into the nearby gas line to service our property.

It turns out the nearby line was actually a different type of gas line which was unsuitable for the application we needed it for. The closest gas line they could tie into was actually two kilometres away and that would come at a cost of nearly fifty thousand dollars, of which Marcy and I would have to pay around twenty thousand dollars for. So here we were again, this time with a service we had budgeted at six thousand dollars now coming in at over twenty thousand.

We had no choice in the matter but to proceed with bringing the utilities in. At a combined total of around forty thousand dollars over budget for major unforeseen issues, we waved goodbye to our plans for a detached garage, because that certainly wasn't going to be happening now, and instead paid the utility companies in full so they could move ahead with the servicing.

This instantly made both Marcy and I very resentful towards our decision to build a house and left us both wishing that we hadn't even tried. This simmering resentment was something that would stay with us both for the next three or four years before we finally accepted everything that had happened and got on with our lives.

Our monthly mortgage payment also increased at the time repayment began because of the additional forty thousand dollars that we had to take from the bank to pay for those inflated utility costs. With the house now three quarters complete and our rental agreement ending within three or four months, this was no time to be discouraged, and it was way too late to turn back at that point, so Marcy and I marched on as we always have. We knew we'd figure it out. Upon receipt of payment to the gas company, they were quick in getting the ball rolling on the gas line installation. The story with the electrical company, however, was going to be something completely different.

On a more positive note, I had made a deposit on an upcoming batch of Labrador retrievers, and it was as all this bad news was unfolding that we got a phone call from the breeder and I was informed that our little puppy was officially ready to be picked up.

We were way too busy in our day-to-day lives while we lived in Morinville to be able to commit to having a dog and the twice-a-day walks associated with having one, so until we moved out to the acreage, having a dog wasn't something that we could entertain. Although getting a puppy for the first time proved to be a real eye-opening experience in which, on multiple occasions, I found myself angry, frustrated, and even seriously pissed at that dog, he became an important part of our lives, and the sixth member of our family.

His name was Jack and he was good boy. He represented the freedom Marcy and I had been seeking by moving out to an acreage to begin with.

In day-to-day life, tensions between Edward and I were still on the rise however, and the arguments were more frequent and more drawn out than they had ever been, and it was starting to take its toll on the mental health of everybody else in the house. I decided to go ahead and reinstate the counselling we had been undertaking before, hoping to get to the bottom of whatever was going on.

Following the closure of the counselling office we had attended a couple years earlier, we would now have to drive to St. Albert and begin the sessions with a different councillor. This was going to be a bit of a game changer in the sense of the commitment required on my end. I would now have to start booking half-days off work to be able to attend the appointments and keep things rolling. Nevertheless, I was prepared to do whatever was necessary to ensure that I saw everything through.

The new councillor Edward was seeing was alright. He definitely wasn't as good as Warren had been, but we saw him anyways, religiously, for a good chunk of that year. As a matter of fact, when summer drew around that year, I had no vacation days left because I had used up all three weeks of my vacation over the course of the year in half-day increments getting Edward into St. Albert for his appointments.

Again, even after all those counselling sessions, medication, and even a psychiatric evaluation, nothing changed, not one damn thing. Even after all this time, he was still hell-bent on moving back in with Ashley.

Twenty-eight

At this point, we were within weeks of taking possession of our new house, and in preparation, Marcy and I had started packing and cleaning up the rental we had been living in.

As per any landlord/tenant agreement, we had to provide one month's notice to the landlord so they could begin the process of locating another renter. This meant that we had to have everything complete at the new house, including the occupancy inspection and approval, all prior to the date we agreed we would vacate the premises. Everything at the new house had turned out really well and was ready to go except one thing, and it was a big one.

We still didn't have any power to the property.

They hadn't even started yet actually. The power provider was faced with two issues on their end that had really held the process up. The first issue was that there were two underground pipelines that needed to be crossed to get that power service to our house, and getting the go ahead from the pipeline companies required a lot of leg work. Both pipeline companies had policies in place that required special equipment to be used for the excavation and backfill around their lines and also stated that their staff were required to be on-site during the time this work was taking place.

The other issue was the farmer who owned the land they wanted to use to trench the power service to our property.

Although this had no impact to him whatsoever, he chose to use this opportunity to his advantage to obtain some free work from the power company moving some poles and wires around on his farm prior to signing his consent for the power company to proceed. I pointed out to the power company that we were moving in within a couple of weeks and that they needed to figure out how to get us temporary power until such time permanent power arrived. When move day finally arrived, our power provider showed up with a small gas-powered generator, tied that into the power meter, and left. This really took the glow off moving into our brand-new house to say the least.

The generator worked of course, but we couldn't use everything we needed to at one time or it would just pop the breaker, and I'd have to go outside and reset it. On top of that, that generator had to run 24/7 to keep the fridge going, so we had to fill it twice a day or it would run out of fuel. The power company was picking up the costs of any fuel we were burning, of course, but we still had the inconvenience of going to the gas station daily, filling up the jerry cans, bringing them home, and filling the generator up. It was ridiculous.

After voicing our complaints to the power company about the undersized generator, they rented us an eight-kilowatt diesel powered monster and tied *that* into the meter instead. It was much better for sure. It didn't alleviate the necessity of having to go to the gas station every day to get fuel to fill it up, but at least it only had to be filled once a day instead of twice, and it had no problem meeting any of the power demands of our house and whatever we were using inside. At a fuel cost of fifty dollars a day for diesel—this would be our power source to our house for the next few months until they finally got that power service to our property.

Even after moving into our new home, the work had literally only just begun, and it was overwhelming how much was still left to do. Investment of time to complete things wasn't the issue though, finances or lack thereof was the problem. Due to how badly we had been left financially with all the unseen, unplanned events that had gone down with the utility companies, trying to finish everything off to produce a complete house with the money we had available wasn't going to be possible. This would include unfinished landscaping, no decks, and of course no garage.

Imagine building a brand-new house, and upon completion, it doesn't have a sidewalk or even a single hard surface anywhere on the property—instead it has a dirt pathway that is damp and muddy half the time leading up to the house. At the main entrance, you are met with a makeshift set of stairs in the place of an inviting deck to get into the house. The front centre of the house boasts a large cavity where another deck *should* be but offers nothing more than a four-foot drop out the front door into a pocket backfilled with dirt and clay. The back of the house reveals a single deck header attached to the wall ready and willing to accept the construction of a thirty-five by twelve-foot deck, but that's all it is... just a single board fastened to the wall with the potential to be so much more. Left over piles of dirt and clay from the basement excavation are scattered around the entire yard waiting to be leveled into their final resting place. A yard devoid of even a single blade of fresh green grass yet busy with many different types of aggressive weeds spreading like wildfire and taking over every square inch of the property.

It's not pretty, is it? But that's where we were.

Our improperly constructed "driveway" was made of nothing more than an abomination of marginal materials all mixed together and frequently became near impassable after any significant precipitation. This was the reality that Marcy and I would live with for the next four or so years. Initially, we thought we might try to sell the place to get out from under it, but as with any new acreage, this too was simply a work in progress, and its true value could only be realized with time. The year before we built our house, the farmers in the area had harvested crops from right where our house now sat. With no grass, frequent mud, and one-foot tall trees around the perimeter of the property that were ten or twelve years away from fulfilling their intended purpose as a shelter belt, our property carried minimal value right out of the gate.

The reality of it was that there wasn't going to be an easy way out from the problems we were now faced with. As disheartening as it had been watching everything unfold the way it did, and as impossible as it was to visualize at the time, this whole undertaking was undoubtedly *not* a failure. We just needed to sit tight and plug away at the things that needed to get done, one-by-one. It was going to take time. Thankfully, if nothing else, time was something we actually had.

I've always known that, down the road, long after everything is completed and Marcy and I are ready to move on, things will come full circle for us and we will get back everything that we invested into the place and then some. This took the sting out of the situation. Still there was a lot of work to do.

I had started the framing process in the basement almost immediately after we had moved in due to the dire need of producing the one bedroom that we were short. Marcy and I had established a pretty awesome floorplan for the basement that included two oversized bedrooms for Josh and Edward and a design that would maximize the use of the rest of the space that we had available.

Bringing that vision to life though would prove daunting. It was going to be a tedious endeavour, and just the framing alone would take a few months to complete. By this time I was starting to feel as though the only time I was communicating with my parents was when I needed something. Because of this I opted out of my default call to my dad to assist me with the framing this time around and ended up completing the majority of it myself instead.

I did end up getting my dad to come help me with a couple ceilings simply because I needed his expertise near the end, but that was about it. I just didn't want my parents feeling as though

I was using them—because that was not the case. I was just super busy being super busy.

The yard was the other major undertaking that Marcy and I immediately embarked on in that first year, shortly after moving in. With not one single hard surface leading up to the entry of the house, the amount of dirt and mud making its way inside anytime it would rain was absolutely ridiculous.

The first major rainfall we experienced after moving into the house was when it first came to light that our driveway had been improperly constructed. After a few hours of rain that night I was on my way out, and as I was walking to my vehicle, I stepped onto the driveway and my foot sunk three inches into an extremely muddy mixture of topsoil, clay, sand, and gravel. Then when I started to back the car up, it almost seemed like I was driving on ice or something as the tires were spinning free and the car was sliding around uncontrollably on the driveway. I was positive I was going to get stuck.

Looking back down the driveway after reaching the road, I could clearly see two deep ruts from my car down the entire length of the driveway caused from me backing out. The driveway had taken on the composition of a very soft yet tacky mixture along its entire length, which is the state it would morph into *anytime* it received precipitation in any measurable amount. Once wet, it would stay that way for days until it had time to dry out again and would then revert back with the next rain. Whatever the material composition of the driveway was, it made a mess of absolutely anything it came into contact with.

Our vehicles were absolutely plastered with it inside and out. Every piece of footwear we owned was covered in it. It would get on our pants and other clothing, and whatever was being tracked inside the house had slowly started taking its toll on all the surfaces throughout as well. It was a horrible situation.

During that first summer, between the basement and the yard issues, it was a constant balancing act as to where our time was more crucially needed—both those undertakings were very important. We knew that during the summer months we could throttle back slightly on the basement development because, when winter arrived, we could then focus all of our efforts there, so we tried to invest as much of our spare time into the yard as possible.

Truthfully though, due to the lack of resources available to us at the time and the high cost of landscaping labour and materials, there wasn't a whole bunch we could really do other than just trying to keep on top of everything that was growing in the yard before it could grow too big to manage. Marcy's parents had purchased us a used lawn tractor as a housewarming gift, and that thing made all the difference in the world in helping to prevent a complete take-over of everything growing in the yard. It was pretty much an hour a day of cutting at that time just to keep on top of it.

Then one day, as I was cutting away, the tractor just died right out of the blue. And just like that, the bitch wouldn't start again. Seeing as I'm not the best when it comes to engines and fixing things mechanically, I started with the obvious stuff but quickly came to the conclusion that this wasn't something simple, something that I was going to be able to diagnose or fix. I had no choice in the interim but to start cutting everything with the push mower until we could get the tractor fixed.

Even at two solid hours a night with that push mower, I could not keep up with the growth that was occurring daily around the yard. After spending a bunch of money on parts and labour trying to fix the tractor, to no avail, it was clear that it made absolutely no sense to spend one more minute or one more dollar trying any further. It was right then and there that we officially lost control of the yard situation, and in no time at all we had a plethora of different weeds, some three feet high, growing across the entire property.

The yard work and equipment needed to live on an acreage like ours was something that had completely escaped our minds during this whole undertaking. We had no idea what we were up against and how quickly it could get out of hand. We had no choice for the remainder of that summer but to live with the situation and try to contain it as best we could.

Twenty-nine

As fall set in that year, we were in the process of completing the framing in the basement, and the time had come to make preparations for the drywall.

This was the first major purchase linked to the development of the basement—everything else thus far had just been little purchases here and there as we went along. Unfortunately, we were about to encounter a problem that actually stemmed back to a decision I had made whilst ordering the windows for the basement way back when during the construction stage. These were fairly large basement windows at roughly three feet by five feet, and when the manufacturer gave me the available options, without really thinking about it at the time, I chose a slider type with one side permanently fixed, and then didn't think anything more about it.

There was one problem.

The fixed portion now meant that, even with the slider portion of the window removed, there was no way to get a sheet of drywall through it. Had it not been for that, getting the one hundred and sixty odd sheets of drywall into the basement would have taken the drywall delivery guys two hours, at most, and wouldn't have been an issue whatsoever. It wasn't until the drywall actually arrived at our house that we discovered the problem with the windows.

What ended up happening was we had to bring the sheets into the house through the main door and take them down the stairs into the basement. This was a lot of work as the stairs went down a half flight, then came to a landing, turned one hundred and eighty degrees, and then down another half flight into the basement. With over a hundred twelve-foot sheets alone in the arsenal of the one hundred and sixty sheets that had arrived, this turned into quite the undertaking. It took three guys—one of whom was me—two days to unload those sheets and get them placed into the basement. I ended up having to take a couple days off work to accommodate these guys in getting the sheets downstairs where they needed to go without destroying everything upstairs in the process.

I immediately began the task of hanging drywall downstairs, but due to the configuration of the basement and all the rooms within it, this was a sizable undertaking. Both our families helped out as much as possible, and slowly but surely, within a few months we had everything boarded out and ready for taping.

We found a taper and gave him the go ahead to get after it and get it all done. When the taping had been completed, Marcy and I painted all the doors, and I installed them. We then primed and painted the walls coming down the stairs into the basement, the hallway leading up to the new bedrooms, and both the kids' rooms. Carol and Henry, in their endless support, paid for the carpet in the stairwell, the carpet down the hallway, and the carpet throughout both kids' rooms as a housewarming gift. That was quickly followed by me installing the baseboards and casings throughout all the areas that we had painted. We ended up closing any doors leading to still unfinished areas of the basement which created a very nice comfortable space leading up to and into the kids' new bedrooms.

After years of battling the same issue, the shortage of bedrooms had yet again been resolved, only this time it was different, because it was once and for all. I felt a massive weight lifted off my shoulders, knowing that I would never have to think about it again. Without the support that we had received from both sides of our family, we would never have been able to complete it. They were instrumental in helping us achieve what we so badly needed to get done.

It was right around this time that Marcy and I were about to receive life changing news yet again.

I remember leaving work early one day, and when I got home, Marcy was in the bathroom. As I was walking by, I could hear her talking to herself, and it sounded like she was really freaking out about something. I wasn't sure what was going on, so I went about my business, and when I returned a few minutes later she was in the kitchen, but she didn't say a word about anything, so I left it alone.

Later that night, when we were lying in bed together, she told me what was going on. She was pregnant and she had literally only found out seconds before I had walked through the door that day.

Seeing as Marcy had now been living with four boys for quite some time (five boys if you count Jack), maybe this would be her chance to have the little girl that she had always dreamt of. I knew she felt the same way that I did about all this, and she was just seeking affirmation from me to reinforce that we could handle this and that we were good to go. We now had enough bedrooms in our house to accommodate everybody—we *already* had plus one more, so in all honesty, we were both pretty excited about it.

Thirty

During all the months that we had been swamped dealing with all the different things going on in our lives, the situation with Ashley as per usual still hadn't changed whatsoever. She hadn't contributed any additional funds towards Josh and Edward and was still very much holding to her position that she would not be held financially responsible for them in any way, shape, or form.

With everything that was happening with the house, the ongoing costs of raising the kids—not the least of which were the braces for Josh—had now really started to kick the shit out of the balance in our bank account, which left me with no choice but to begin putting in extra hours wherever possible just to keep on top of things.

I was sick and tired of the way Marcy and I had to work so hard to cover all costs associated with Josh and Edward while their biological mother couldn't be bothered to contribute a single thing, so I decided to threaten her with legal action if she didn't start paying some type of child support.

She literally responded with a text laughing and telling me I would never get a ruling from a court because she had no income, and therefore, there was no money to take from. After talking with Carol about it, she was in agreement that something needed to be done.

Once again, as much as I was dreading to have to do it, I knew that I was going to have to borrow the money from Henry and Carol to retain that representation in court. As for Ashley though, and as per usual, she wouldn't have to pay a damn thing. We tried to hire Sylvia again but as it turned out she had since retired and was no longer available, so we were referred to Rob Smith who had taken her place at the firm.

After sitting down with him and discussing all the details of what had been happening, he couldn't believe it, and he was more than ready to nail her to the cross, but he suggested that, before we went ahead and spent a bunch of money trying to resolve this, we try mediation first. I really didn't want to do the whole mediation thing again—previously it had been a complete waste of time. Obviously, mediation only works if the people involved in it stand behind what they are agreeing to, and as history had shown time and time again, Ashley was not the type of person who would stand behind anything that she said.

But in an attempt to save the money that I didn't even have to begin with, I went ahead and booked the mediation anyways. In truth, I was dreading the whole process because I could hardly stand being in a room with Ashley anymore not to mention having to listen to her talk. When the mediation day arrived, the session I had to endure consisted of the same type of bullshit as all the other times I had gone through this. The mediator was very cautious the way she confronted Ashley regarding the issues that we were there to discuss.

Instead of calling it for what it was and telling Ashley straight-up that she needed to start contributing to the costs of raising her children, she would instead pussy foot around everything. One part of the mediation that sticks out in my mind to this day:

"Ashley," the mediator said, "I know you're a great mom, and you only want the best for your kids, so do you think you could provide three hundred dollars a month for your children?"

Ashley said that she had just recently finished up some schooling and wasn't finding any success in landing a job since completion of her course, and therefore, had no money to contribute.

"Well, have you considered finding interim work, like a retail job or even something at a fast food chain? This is what people do while they are waiting to land work in a field for which they've trained."

Ashley claimed (lied probably) that she'd applied at numerous fast food restaurants but that she was overqualified for that type of job, and therefore, they wouldn't hire her.

Yeah, she actually said that.

By the end of that mediation session, the ball was in my court now, and the mediator was asking me if I was willing to agree to a lower monthly payment amount than what was listed in the child support calculation tables. At that point, I agreed I would accept two hundred dollars a month as Ashley's child support contribution to the kids because it was better than nothing, and Marcy and I needed the help.

Ashley agreed.

I wasn't happy with the agreement that was made that day, I felt it was unfair, but in my mind, I decided it was better than nothing, so I signed off on it. As I mentioned above, a mediation is only as good as the word of the people agreeing to the terms within it, and almost immediately, after we had signed off on everything, it became clear Ashley had no intention of honouring her end of the deal.

No payment from Ashley meant that in no time at all I found myself back in Rob's office paying the retainer and giving him the go-ahead to start court proceedings for child support. He wasted no time in getting the ball rolling doing just that.

Over the next couple months, the court date for child support was set, the lawyers going back and forth discussing details. About ten days before the court date, I received a call from Rob out of the blue one day. He had called to schedule an urgent meeting with me.

Upon arriving at his office, he proceeded to sit me down and inform me that he was resigning from my case, actually he was resigning from all his cases, due to an adverse health condition that he had recently been diagnosed with. Ten days from court that news hit me pretty hard.

Rob gave me the name of the lawyer who would be picking up the pieces of his cases, a guy by the name of Brent Lougheed. He gave me all of my paperwork that had been filed with the court, shook my hand, wished me luck and said goodbye. I quickly made an appointment to meet Brent as time was of the essence, and once I was sitting down with him the first thing he told me was that he was going to need a retainer in place prior to looking at my case.

I knew right then and there that I was fucked and that I would now be representing myself in court. When I got home and started looking through all the paperwork that Rob had given me, there was a cheque for the remaining funds left over from the retainer that Carol and Henry had given me initially. Fifty percent of those funds had already been depleted just in the paperwork and phone calls. I gave that cheque back to Carol and Henry feeling like nothing shy of a complete failure because, other than wasting a bunch of money, nothing else had been accomplished here.

Truthfully, this was really nothing shy of a disaster. At that point, I began the process of trying to prepare myself as best as I could for a court date set to arrive in just a week or so. When that day arrived, I was up early as I had been suffering from some anxiety the last several days regarding the whole ordeal. And the night before I had tossed all night long and hardly caught a wink of sleep in the process.

I knew I was doing the right thing by taking Ashley to court in an attempt to make her responsible for her children—hell, this was something that I should have done nearly three years earlier. In the back of my mind, though, I was still nervous about the outcome. Why though? It's not like I had much to lose. The worst thing that could really happen would be the court not imposing a monthly child support payment on Ashley, and then things would be the same as they had been all along.

Perhaps my anxiety in all this had stemmed from the money and resources that had been dumped into getting us nowhere. To my pleasant surprise that morning, Marcy told me that she had also taken the day off work and was going to accompany me to court that day. Just knowing that she was going to be there with me helped to take the edge off everything I was feeling.

Ashley didn't even bother to show up in court that day. I guess she didn't have to as her legal aid lawyer was there in her place. When our time arrived to be heard by the judge, it came to light almost immediately that Ashley had failed to provide the court with all the required financial information regarding her income from the previous two years.

Her lawyer began making excuses to the judge as to why those documents hadn't been provided as of yet, and he was trying to get another court date set to address things later. As it turned out, the judge had a very low tolerance for bullshit, and she shut him down in under a minute.

She had the wrath of god in her eyes as she told Ashley's lawyer that Ashley was responsible to pay child support for her children and that it was inexcusable that she hadn't been. She immediately placed a three hundred and fifty dollar a month payment on Ashley and said it would stand until the proper financial forms made their way to the court at which time it could be adjusted accordingly.

The judge also demanded Ashley backpay me for three months of support, as well as a one-time fee of one hundred and twenty dollars to cover some of the wages I had lost in having to attend court that day. In my mind this was a win—at long last, Ashley would finally be held responsible and forced to contribute to her kids at a monitored legal level.

I still wasn't a hundred percent sold on the fact that Ashley would now start to make that monthly payment solely based on a court ordering her to do so, and after some discussion with Marcy, I decided the best thing I could do was to stop off and register the new child support agreement with the maintenance enforcement program. That way if Ashley did choose not to make her payments, or she was late making them, it wouldn't be something that I would have to deal with, it would instead be handled by maintenance enforcement.

I was really looking forward to the relief that a few extra dollars a month from Ashley would provide to Marcy and me in our household, but as the story will tell, that relief would never arrive.

When that first payment came due, Ashley failed to make it.

I talked to maintenance enforcement and they informed me that they had already placed a call to her and were awaiting a response for confirmation as to when they could expect to see those funds paid in full. It would be several months before I would talk with maintenance enforcement again, and during that time, not one single penny from Ashley would ever be deposited into my bank account.

Thirty-one

Flash forward a few months to the end of August 2014 and the much-anticipated arrival of Anna, the most beautiful little girl that I have ever laid eyes on was upon us. She had finally come into the world and, in the process, had changed my view on everything kid-related that I had ever known. Three boys and one little girl would mark the completion of our family forever.

These were extremely busy times for us having four kids—one a baby—so there was quite a bit of planning involved to keep things around the house running as smoothly as possibly. Back on the home front, Randy and Lyla had come to the rescue with regards to the issues in our yard that had returned with spring a few months previous.

They had access to some heavy-duty agricultural type equipment, which they had brought out to help us take back control of our yard. Initially, before we had built the house, Marcy and her friend had planted several hundred trees around the perimeter of the property, and because they were so tiny, they had become lost in the all the weeds that had grown in, and sadly we were going to lose a ton of them just trying to get everything in the yard turned with discs and ready for grass seed.

After many hours of hard work from all parties involved, everything had been cut, turned, seeded and flattened, and the nightmare yard we had been dealing with since the day we had moved in was now nothing more than a memory. The driveway, however... well that was a nightmare that was going to last for a couple more years into the future yet. But a success is a success, and we happy to put this one in the books as so.

By this time, day-to-day life in our home was becoming more dysfunctional than ever between Edward and I, and that was making life for everybody else in the house harder than ever also. It had gotten to a point where I couldn't even get him to take a shower without literally having to argue with him for fifteen or twenty minutes before he would finally do it (I'm not exaggerating).

We would sit at the table for two sometimes three hours doing homework that would have taken twenty minutes if he had just done the work, and we'd be going at each other that entire time. The negativity generated by the constant fighting and arguing between us had, ever so slowly, began to poison the atmosphere in our home. I didn't see this happening, of course, because I was in the thick of it all, but it was slowly taking hold of everybody in one form or another, and it had the potential to rip us apart.

These daily interactions over the next several months between Edward and I were exhausting to say the least. From morning until night, it was a constant battle, day in and day out, and nothing I was doing on the sidelines seemed to change anything. Eventually, due to the lack of any measurable improvement, I opted to remove Edward from the counselling, from the meds, and from everything else. All that extra work, time, and money spent for two plus years had literally made no difference whatsoever.

With zero results yielded, it had never been clearer to me that this had been nothing more than wasted time and resources. Believe me when I tell you that there was nothing more that I wanted in this world than to get Edward the help he needed to crawl out of his shell, and there wasn't anything I wouldn't have given to help him achieve that, but he just wouldn't have it.

Going back to the whole maintenance enforcement ordeal, it had now been almost eight months since I'd had any communication and I still hadn't seen a single penny deposited into my bank account from Ashley over that time. I decided to reach out to them and see what was going on with all of it.

One thing can be said about the maintenance enforcement program, regardless of what side of the system you're on—be it debtor or a creditor—the whole process is convoluted. When I called in to inquire about the status of my account, I was put on hold for about five minutes until such time the system kicked me to a voicemail and instructed me to leave my information for a call back.

When they did call me back, they had a wealth of information to tell me about the account as they had been documenting everything in great detail since I had registered it two thirds of a year earlier, and that documentation told the whole story. Ashley hadn't made a single payment to date. and the maintenance enforcement program had been placing different restrictions on her to try and get her to follow through with her court ordered obligation.

Initially they had started with a wage garnishment, but when somebody doesn't maintain steady employment, it becomes difficult to garnish wages from them. They had then proceeded to report derogatory credit to her file at the credit bureau and had also began to monitor any government payments scheduled to be released to her that they could latch onto as well.

It also appeared that, right around that time, they had also suspended any and all services from government registries which would prevent her from being able to renew her driver's license or car registration or any other dealings related to needing a registry. And yet despite all that, she still hadn't made even one single payment.

Thirty-two

As it would turn out, with the obvious pressure Ashley was likely feeling from maintenance enforcement clamping down on her, and the massive amount of debt building in child support arrears against her, the gears in her head had started to turn, and she began to engineer a plan to change the status quo.

It was sometime in April 2015 when things between Edward and I had finally came to a head. With three months of school left I wanted him to start investing some time in studying so he could finish the year off with a bang.

But he wouldn't do it.

His marks had been extremely low all year long, and I thought that if he was prepped for his final exams, it would be a perfect opportunity for him to achieve some stronger final marks or at least get him to the point of passing anyways.

It was about ten o'clock one night, we had been arguing at the table for a few hours at that point, and I was done with it. I'd had enough. I told him to go have a shower and get to bed. As per usual, even the simple act of having a shower was something that he wanted to fight and argue about, so I ended up telling him to just to go to bed.

He crawled into his bed with no shower, without brushing his teeth, and completely dirty from the day's activities. I told him I was pissed off and tired of all this bullshit day in and day out and when I slammed his light switch off and was walking away down the hallway to head back upstairs, I heard him let out a laugh.

"Fucker."

That was Edward, age thirteen—a direct quote by the way—and it was right then and there that I had reached the end of my rope. The line had now been crossed. Over the years, with Edward and Josh, I found myself stuck so many times struggling to try and quickly determine the best way to deal with scenarios like this and coming up blank almost every time.

I have never been one to take any bullshit from my kids, nor I have ever been one to respond to their bullshit in a physical manner—and they know that—but that night as I whipped around and headed back to Edward's room in response to what had just been said to me, I think both he and Josh were on edge about what the hell might be about to go down.

They had likely both anticipated that something physical was going to ensue, and truthfully as severely pissed off as I was, I was in complete control of myself and my actions. Josh tried to intervene as I walked past him in the hallway—I told him to mind his own business, and as I entered Edward's room I closed the door behind me.

In my mind, at that moment in time, my only priority was in delivering a message to Edward loud and clear that I would never accept that type of behaviour from him. When I got back in his room I got right in his face and I had raised my voice to him and I kept him telling him over and over to say it again, I dared him to. We were going back and forth, and at one point I jabbed him in the chest with my finger. Poked him. My intent in all this certainly wasn't to physically harm him or be abusive towards him. I was simply a parent at the end of his tether trying desperately to reach a kid who was, in turn, trying to remain stubbornly unreachable.

I certainly never wanted to play a role like Ashley had in the sense of transmitting a bunch of unnecessary stress and anxiety to any of my kids, and I always tried my best not to, but unfortunately it was during times like these, through my actions, that I may have done just that. While all this was going on, Josh had taken it upon himself to call Ashley and report to her the state of events underway at my house at that moment.

So in the middle of this dispute, my phone starts ringing, and it's Ashley and she's calling because she wants to know what the hell is going on. This may sound like a concerned mother trying to protect her children, but I can assure you that was not the case here whatsoever. The only person between the two of us who ever had the kids' well-being in mind was me. Ashley wasn't looking at this as a crisis—this was nothing more than an opportunity.

Keep in mind that this is a mother of four who had already abandoned her two younger children when she had divorced from Dave a few years back. She had then taken a hiatus of nearly four years from all her kids during which time she had dragged six or eight different guys in and out of their lives (one of whom was deemed dangerous by the authorities). She also minimized the amount of time that she spent with any of her kids and paid absolutely nothing in child support.

Does any of that sound like a mother who has ever cared about the well-being of her children?

And now she had called me to express her concerns about my parenting style? She didn't have the slightest clue as to what was going on in this or any other aspect of the kids' lives. It was too little, too late and I didn't give a fuck what she had to say. As far as I was concerned, she didn't even have an opinion in any of this and I told her that.

After everything was said and done, I went upstairs to go to bed, and I was met there by Marcy who was anything but happy to see me. The constant arguing and fighting was really starting to take its toll on her, and she didn't want our two younger kids to be exposed to the negativity that had been present around the clock the last couple years.

That night when I did go to bed, sleep for me was far away, and I had a long time to lay there replaying the night's events in my head, wishing I had the ability to change what happened and feeling like a bag of shit about it because I couldn't. I should have known that the intimidation route had been the wrong approach and that I would never get through to him that way.

As previously mentioned, Ashley was looking to change the status quo in an attempt to escape the pressures that maintenance enforcement had been placing on her, and this blow-up between me and Edward would be the opportunity she needed to start laying the groundwork for a plan to do just that.

I overheard a conversation between her with Edward that next day in which she was instructing him that he should try to have me charged with assault. She was telling him that if he called the police and reported that I had assaulted him, basically they could remove him from my care, and he could move back in with her. It was obvious that she was working hard to try and convince him that his life would be so much better if he lived with her again, and that together they could achieve it.

Edward's desire to move back in with his mom hadn't diminished at all over that four-year period, and because he was hell-bent that he would one day move back in with her, I think it was very easy for Ashley to coax him into doing things that she wanted. I confronted him on the conversation I had overheard between him and his mom, and I explained to him that I certainly wasn't worried about being charged with assault for the simple fact that I hadn't assaulted him.

It isn't illegal to discipline your children within reason, and I hadn't done anything even remotely approaching the limits of discipline, and furthermore, that would be obvious to anyone called in to follow up on the accusation. The only concern I had in all this was the fact that his own mother would go so far as to actually plant an idea like that in his mind.

You have to ask yourself: What kind of person is this really? What kind of parent tries to persuade their child to commit character assassination against the other parent? Ashley's only motivation in any of this was financial. This was about getting Edward back full-time so she could call off the enforcement officials.

Though I didn't know it at the time, there were big changes on the horizon, and they were set to dawn in the very near future.

Thirty-three

It all started after Josh and Edward spent a couple days at Ashley's place shortly after the big falling out at home. I received a text from Ashley requesting we meet at a coffee shop that afternoon because there was some things she needed to talk to me about. I knew right then and there that something was up.

Obviously, I didn't know what it was, but after all the years of dealing with Ashley and her relentless mission of trying to screw me over any way possible, it left no doubt in my mind this would likely be something substantial. When I arrived at the coffee shop, Ashley and Edward were waiting for me. After sitting down, she informed me that Edward had something he wanted to talk to me about and she probed him to proceed.

As per usual, she had gone ahead and put my kid right in the middle of something that should have been discussed in a private conversation between us. That's when Edward told me he wanted to move back in with his mom. No surprise there. I asked them both if they had really thought this through fully, and they both assured me that indeed they had. As Edward was only thirteen at the time, I certainly would never had expected him to have the foresight to be able to choose what was best for himself in the long term.

I knew his decision in wanting to move out was based entirely on the ideas that Ashley had put into his mind—cake and lollipops. I explained to them both that I felt going ahead with this was going to be a mistake because they hadn't lived together for a very long time at that point, and realistically, neither of them was the same person that they remembered living with all those years earlier. I could certainly vouch that was the truth for Edward anyways. Any memories that Ashley had living with him in previous years were nothing more than just that.

That sweet little innocent boy had evolved into something much different at this point. His personality had become complex, and Ashley had no idea how hard day-to-day life with him could really get. That didn't matter, though; they had clearly already made this decision together prior to announcing it to me anyways, and whatever I had to say about it now was neither here nor there. I asked Ashley what kind of timeframe she had in mind if this transition was to take place, and she said she wanted to take him immediately.

She claimed she would drive him to his current school out where we lived every day until the end of the year and look after any other details in the interim. I knew in my mind—from a legal perspective—there was just no way I could win this if push came to shove. I certainly didn't have the money or resources available if a court battle was to ensue and because it wouldn't cost her a dime, I was once again beat in this before I had even begun.

I told Ashley that there was no way that I would let him go before the end of that school year, and that was final. With only a couple of months left, he would first have to fulfill his commitments on my end, and then I guess, at that point, I would have no choice but to let him go—even though I knew I was only setting him up for failure by doing so. Had I agreed to let Ashley take him that day, who knows what the outcome with the rest of that school year would've been.

Within a couple days of this new information surfacing, Marcy and I had a couple discussions about what was happening, and we decided it was important and necessary to call a family meeting between us and Edward. We wanted a chance to sit down *without* Ashley present to give him a chance to talk and see exactly what it was that he wanted in all this. Edward was quick to stand by his decision and insist he indeed wanted to go live with Ashley. I wanted to verify that he had in fact been made aware of all the variables that would come with moving away.

One of those things which in my mind was the biggest one was that he would once again have to start a new school. After four years of attending the same school with the same kids, he'd have to start all over again. This time, however, seeing as he would now be residing in Edmonton, he would have to attend a school with five times the student population of the school he was used to attending. I reminded him that he had four years left until completion of high school, and then his life was his own to do with as he wanted. But nothing I could say would change anything.

He was on his way out the door, and that was that.

All the chaos, turmoil, and changes occurring in my home at that time were all because of Ashley, and once again, because of her actions, my kids would soon be separated from each other in their day-to-day lives, just as they had been in the past, and only see each other on weekends. Due to the fact that I was backed into a corner, metaphorically speaking, I agreed that I would sign off full custody of Edward to Ashley during the upcoming summer break of 2015.

That was a hard thing to come to terms with and not a decision that I took lightly. It was disheartening not only for the fact that Edward would no longer be living under my roof where I knew his basic needs were being met, but primarily because I knew that his future had undoubtedly been compromised in all this. This was nothing more than the final installment of a plan that Ashley had been engineering over the last few months, one that had finally reached maturity.

Sadly, it had absolutely nothing to do with her ability to provide Edward with a better life or a better opportunity because, quite simply, she couldn't. Her motive behind everything she had done was simply a means to escape from the massive debt she had run up with maintenance enforcement from non-payment of child support for our kids. Because the parenting agreement between Ashley and I would soon need to be altered to reflect the change of custody come summer time, the child support payments would then also have to be modified at that same time to accommodate that arrangement as well, and getting things to that point was the basis of Ashley's plan right from the go.

Some quick calculations from the child support tables revealed that, with the income I had, I would be required to pay Ashley nearly eight hundred dollars a month in change for Edward. And for her part, with the income she had, she would be required to pay me about one hundred and seventy five for Josh. Once those payments offset it would leave me with a six hundred dollar a month ongoing payment to her. Ashley booked the court date so that the custody and child support documents could be written up in advance to reflect the changes that would be taking place later that summer.

I was curious to see how the court was going to respond to the outrageous amount of *outstanding* child support Ashley owed to me, and perhaps more importantly, what the judge might take away from the fact that she hadn't bothered to make one single payment to me ever, and that included since being ordered to do so by the court.

When that court date arrived, there was no mention of wrongdoing on her part whatsoever.

The judge looked over everything that had been submitted, including the tentative custody agreement, deemed it acceptable by the court, and approved it. The three thousand dollars in child support arrears that Ashley had failed to pay to me over the course of the previous year would now be squared away in a similar fashion as to when I had overpaid her thousands in support a few years previous. She would simply do without payments until the debt was paid in full.

Thirty-four

Following this latest bout of legal rigmarole, the days that had been passing one by one quickly became weeks and, before I knew it, *months*—and suddenly the school year had ended, and the day that I had been dreading had inevitably arrived.

As per the custody agreement Ashley and I had recently made in court, one morning in August of 2015, Edward was scheduled to move out of our house and move back in with Ashley at which point she would have full custody and control of him. I knew when I woke up that morning that this wasn't going be an easy day for me, and I wasn't looking forward to it at all. I had already been forced once to say goodbye to both Josh and Edward years back when Ashley had moved them to Red Deer without telling me, and I had never forgotten how hard it was to do that.

Now I was going to have to do it again, but this time it felt as though it was worse because I had known for months in advance exactly when this day was going to arrive, and now here it was. On top of that, I also had to come to grips with the fact that had I never bothered to pursue Ashley for child support in the first place, things undoubtedly would have been different.

That was a bitter pill to swallow.

Every single event that had occurred leading up to the moment she had once again legally taken custody of Edward was linked to child support—either past, present, or future—and her desire to ensure she was the one on the receiving end of it.

If Ashley had taken Edward back into her custody because she was capable of doing a better job of parenting than I was, then I'd have been fine with it. If she could have provided him with a better lifestyle or better opportunities than me, then fine, I would have been alright with that too. But Ashley taking custody of Edward simply to ensure that the government could not hold her responsible for child support… well that was just wrong, especially considering the fact that she didn't have the means to look after him properly anyways.

When Ashley arrived that day to pick Edward up, they were quick in loading up the belongings he was taking with him and then without saying a single word to me, Marcy, or anybody else.

He jumped into her car, and they drove off.

He didn't say goodbye, so long, or even fuck off for that matter. Instead he chose to said nothing at all, and truthfully, for me it was heartbreaking as I watched him drive away that day.

Despite the sadness and despair that had filled me when he did leave, it soon came to light that his departure had also carried with it a silver lining. In truth, had Ashley not taken him away from us when she did, much bigger problems could have unfolded in my home shortly thereafter with devastating consequence to everyone else in our family. By the time Ashley had removed Edward from our custody, Marcy had let me know, on more than one occasion, of her growing unhappiness with all the negativity being generated by the constant battling between him and I.

Her concerns as to the impact it may have on our little ones over time had grown, and quite frankly, she just couldn't live with it anymore. She was at the end of her rope and—although I didn't know this at that time—she had begun to investigate what options she potentially had available to her if necessary, including the possibility of leaving with our two kids just to escape it all. It was nothing more than Ashley's impatience in being unable to wait to tip the scales in her direction so she could screw me over once again that literally saved my marriage.

Following his departure, Edward was front and centre in my mind almost around the clock. I couldn't help but wonder how he was doing in the new life he had chosen for himself or what the future now held for him, considering the circumstances that had led to his move to begin with. I was actually quite worried about him after he had left. He had gone from living on a quiet acreage located outside a small town with a population of under ten thousand people—and under my watchful eye—to living in a major city with a population of nearly a million people and almost complete freedom.

From one extreme to the other, and I was worried that Ashley's hands-off parenting (if you could even call it parenting) would mean he'd simply get lost in the hustle bustle of the big city. But really what could I do about it? It had been made clear to me by both Ashley and Edward that my opinion held no value whatsoever. My parenting time with Edward dwindled to four days a month, and that was only if he'd even come home at all.

Ashley had no intention of supporting or encouraging him to have a relationship with me in the future, so instead of expressing concern to him as to the importance of he and I maintaining a relationship—as any responsible parent would—she instead supported him in his decision not to.

Upon reaching the realization that everything Marcy and I had endured and sacrificed over those four years when it came to Edward had been for absolutely nothing, I knew the time had come that I needed to distance myself from all this bullshit and concentrate on the many other things in my life that were equally important—like my *other* three kids. I had no intention of ever completely exiting Edward's life, of course; I'd always be there for him if he needed me, and I planted that seed in his head a few times leading up to the day that he had left—and meant it. I had full intentions of staying involved as much as I could without allowing it to consume me as it had before.

As far as Ashley went, I expected at a bare minimum that she would keep me in the loop as to how things were going with Edward in general, but as I found out shortly after he left, she had no intention of giving me a glimpse into her dysfunctional life or any of the things inside it whether it involved him or not. I was always the last one to be notified about any events occurring in his life—if I was even notified at all, which often I wasn't. There were a lot of secrets being kept from me regarding Edward, and the bigger the issue, the more secretive Ashley was about it. She would give Edward a strict directive to not reveal any information to me about anything during our weekends together.

In those first two years, nearly anything that I did find out about, whether it was something currently happening at the time or something that had already taken place, would typically come to me through Josh be it accidentally or through concern for Edward's well-being.

Thirty-five

Back at home there was still an undeniable change in the overall atmosphere of our house once Edward moved out. It was much quieter and way more laid-back than it had been in a very long time, and I think everybody was recuperating from the years long battle that had finally come to an end. In truth, everything that had been happening around home up until that point had felt a lot like walls slowly closing in around me, almost as if I was suffocating.

As relieved as I was, however, that none of us had to endure that extra stress, I was still distraught at the thought of what could go wrong with Edward now that he was no longer under our care. My instincts have never let me down when it came to my kids, and this would be no exception. I knew that the outcome of all this—based simply on the reasoning that had set everything in motion to begin with—wasn't going to be good.

In all honesty though, I didn't think that Ashley would let it go to the extreme that she eventually did. When Edward moved back in with Ashley, she had been living with a guy that she'd been dating for a while. A guy named Mark. And these were some of the most stable times that I had ever seen her have. They still moved around a bit, but it was nothing like what Ashley had been doing in all the years prior. I can honestly say, for the most part, I didn't mind Mark. Josh and Edward didn't seem to mind him either.

He never once overstepped his boundaries with me regarding the kids like some of Ashley's boyfriends had done over the years, and for me that was huge. Even at different times, when things were getting ugly between Ashley and I, he didn't try to be some hero by getting involved, he left her to fight her own battles with me as he should have.

When the new school year began, Ashley had enrolled Edward in a school close to where they were residing at that time. It was a smaller city school, but it still had twice the student population of the school he had been attending the four years previous. I was really worried about how things were going to go in all this. I knew from those previous four school years just how much effort it took to try and keep him on track with school—if that was even possible at all—and I knew that Ashley wasn't going to invest the necessary time with him. Near the end of that school year, Edward was expelled, and because Ashley refused to keep me in the loop, I had no idea that anything had even transpired. Apparently she didn't feel this little event warranted a phone call to me because I never heard a single word from her about it, and so when I did catch wind that he may no longer be in school, I ended up having to call her to find out if it was true or not and what had occurred if it was.

She informed me that Edward had apparently brought a Swiss Army knife into the school with him one day. I don't know where he got it, but I can safely assure you that his intention certainly wasn't in utilizing it to harm anybody. Nonetheless, the simple act of bringing it into the school with him meant that the damage had been done. Ashley then claimed that it was actually the principal at the school who was the problem in all this—not Edward and *certainly* not her. She claimed this principal didn't like Edward and had been looking for a reason to get rid of him almost from day one and was simply using this opportunity to do just that.

I was in total agreement with the school's views and actions in all this; assuring the safety of all other students was priority one and it made sense that they had chosen the swift approach they did in prohibiting him from attending their school any longer. The only saving grace in any of this was the fact that the school year was very near its end, and he didn't miss very much time due to not being able to finish it out.

Arrangements were made, after his expulsion, that the following school year he would have to start at yet another school. This time it was a massive one with nearly two thousand students in attendance. It made me nervous for him just thinking about it. I grew up in a small town with small schools, and these massive city schools scared the hell out of me when I was a kid and still scared me now that Edward was about to start attending one himself. I guess I was upset because this wasn't the way it had to go. This story could have been so much different, and because of money, it wasn't going to be. Not only was Edward going to have to switch to yet another school, but he was also going to have to do so with a label attached to his name, one that didn't accurately represent the person he actually was.

When the summer holidays arrived shortly thereafter the arrangement was as per usual. Over the course of the four years Marcy and I had custody of both Josh and Edward, when summer vacation rolled around, they would typically both stay with us for the first month and Ashley would take them for the second month—after which they would both return home at the beginning of September so we had time to get them back into their school routine. Once Edward had moved out, that arrangement basically stayed the same except that, when September rolled around, only Josh would come home, and we'd continue doing the same in getting him back into the school routine.

Near the end of that summer in 2016 there was an almost exact repeat of the events that had gone down the previous year, and it started with a call from Josh. He wanted to set up a meeting with me, himself, and his mom. As it turned out, this little meeting was set to take place over at that same local coffee shop where I had learned the year before that Edward was planning to move out. I agreed to the meeting, we set a date on the calendar, and I knew after I hung up the phone with him that this was a repeat of what had happened with Edward the previous year and that instantly gave me some heavy anxiety. I wasn't looking forward to this meeting—as a matter of fact, I was dreading it. I had a discussion with Marcy about it, and she assured me that, no matter what the outcome, we would figure it out together as we always had.

When the day arrived, I was almost beside myself. The tension and anxiety I was suffering from was overwhelming. It wasn't long after I had arrived and sat down with a coffee that Josh let the cat out of the bag—he did indeed want to move back in with Ashley as well. She had a sort of smirk on her face when Josh revealed that information to me, almost like she thought it was funny that she had been successful in not only already taking one of the kids from my custody, but now she had also convinced the other one as well that he would be better off living with her.

The thing Ashley failed to recognize was that Josh was not Edward. As much as this seemed poised to play out like a repeat of the previous summer, it wasn't going to. Josh understood that I had his best interests at heart; he knew that if he followed that lead when I gave it to him, he would find success. I had a different relationship with him, and he was fairly logical with most things, so I put my foot down at this little meeting.

I told them, no fucking way.

I explained to Josh that Marcy and I could provide him anything he could ever possibly need to achieve success in his life and that making the choice to move in with his mom almost guaranteed failure. I also made mention to him that with only two years of school left, it didn't make sense to pull up roots now and start over with a new school, and new people. I knew that he was missing Edward and that was the largest contributing factor in his decision to want to move away and that Ashley had simply been deliberately playing on those emotions as a means to an end.

Because Josh had always been fairly logical when it came to bigger decisions like this, I think he was able to see what the best option was for himself even though it may not have been the one that he truly wanted to take. I was relieved that after some discussion he agreed he would stay put at home with Marcy and me. Inside I was very sad for him because I knew that he was torn and had only been following his heart in all this, and only because of Ashley's willingness to exploit and cash in on that impulse. All I ever wanted was the best for my kids, and yet time and time again, because of Ashley's constant meddling, I found myself in very hard positions having to make tough decisions regarding them.

As per the usual arrangement, at the end of that month, Josh returned home a few days prior to school starting so Marcy and I could begin the process of getting him back into the groove of things. But as I was soon to find out, things with him had changed over the course of that summer, and there were new issues that were now going to have to be dealt with.

Thirty-six

I'll admit I was always uneasy during the summers when Ashley had both Josh and Edward for that one month because she never had any activities planned for them, nor were there any controls in place during that time. Essentially, they ran wild for that month, and it was because of that lack of planning and control that the events of this particular summer were allowed to occur.

Josh was heavy into skateboard-type activities in those days and would spend hours and hours every week just going hard at the skate park perfecting his craft. He would ask me for a ride to our local skate park almost daily, and I would usually drop him off so he could tear it up for a couple hours and burn off some energy. I had no issue with that, I was just happy that he was outside doing physical activity, and I could still keep an eye on the goings on around him.

That being said, my opinion on skate parks is not high.

I like the idea of a place where kids such as mine can go for free to do something that they love. However, skate parks are also completely unsupervised areas where, in my experience, there can be a lot of undesirable behaviour. Anything from foul language to drug use, and these activities occur regardless of any younger children that may be in attendance utilizing the park at the same time.

I've witnessed it. I eventually got to a point where I wouldn't even take Michael or Anna with me when I went to watch Josh at the skate park. Josh had been spending an excessive amount of time daily at a large skate park near Ashley's residence in Edmonton during that summer, and after being offered marijuana time and again, he decided to try it—and from there had begun to use it frequently.

Now I know there are people out there who would just love to argue with me about marijuana and how it's not bad for you. They are quick in trying to back their statements by pointing out the fact that it was just recently legalized for recreational use in Canada border to border. But that's a deliberate simplification of the facts.

This was a problem for a number of reasons. First, marijuana was still illegal at the time all this went down. Second, even if it had been legalized by that point in time, Josh was still under eighteen and by law still could not have legally possessed or used it. And finally, there is the big concern that I had in all this: It has been scientifically proven that up until the age of about twenty-five or so, marijuana has adverse effects on the development of the brain.

Now I realize that kids will be kids. They are curious and easily coaxed into trying things. But this all boiled down to little more than the fact that Josh had too much free time on his hands to do him any good. Any kid with too much unstructured time will eventually find themselves doing something that they shouldn't. Josh was no exception.

Over the course of that month in Edmonton, as the use of this drug was occurring on a daily basis, either Ashley failed to notice Josh was high as a kite every day when he arrived back at her place, or she just didn't care. Frankly one explanation is as likely as the other, and my guess is that it was a little bit of both.

I could tell there was *something* going on upon his return home that summer, and as it turned out it wasn't far into the future that I'd be finding out exactly what it was. In hindsight, leading up to the time that everything did come to light, I can now see the growing trend in Josh's desire to want to spend more and more time on the weekends at Ashley's place instead of at home—the activities he wanted to partake in were very difficult to do at our house because of our location of living out in the country.

One thing that can be said about living on a farm or an acreage is that maintaining control of your kids and their day-to-day activities is far easier when they can't simply step out the door and get into trouble.

As I was heading home one day, I received a call from the principal of Josh's high school. I knew this must be something pretty substantial because, as far as Josh went, I had received maybe one phone call from the school in the entire time that he had been living with us.

The principal informed me that, at the end of the day, as Josh was walking through the school, that he had smelled strongly of marijuana. It was evident he had been smoking it prior to entering the school that day, and with the potent smell that was following him everywhere he went, the principal had quickly grabbed him and at that time had him in custody in the office.

Josh was searched at which point they had found a substantial amount of marijuana stashed away in his pocket. This is where Josh actually caught a break in all this. Through nothing more than dumb luck, the way the situation had been handled at the school allowed him to narrowly escape the potential of being brought up on possession charges that may have hindered him for the rest of his life. Because the principal had been the one who removed the marijuana from Josh's pocket and given it to the police—rather than allowing it to be removed by the police themselves when they arrived—he was not charged with possession.

He did, however, pull a one-week suspension from school, and now that I knew what he had been doing, things in his life were going to change moving forward. In his best interests they had to. I had a couple of follow-up meetings with the principal and learned some interesting things about what had been happening with Josh. The principal made note to me that he had been surprised that upon Josh's return to school that year he had immediately made a complete change of friends.

Apparently, he had stopped associating with his usual clan and had begun to hang around with another group of kids known to the school to be problematic for these exact types of activities. I explained to the principal that I had full intentions of taking any steps necessary to help Josh put this behind him, and that I had, in fact, already begun the process of doing so.

The principal agreed he would keep an eye on Josh during school and contact me with any concerns, and I assured him I would have a close eye on things at home. It was blatantly obvious that the summer arrangement that Ashley and I been utilizing the last few years during summer holidays was no longer going to work—something was going to have to change.

Ashley who claimed no responsibility whatsoever for Josh starting to use marijuana. She claims her lack of supervision was not a contributing factor in any of this. I told Josh that he could still go over to his mom's every second weekend as he always had, but for the foreseeable future he could no longer stay overnight. He could go for one day during that weekend and then he'd have to come home that night.

Due to the amount of driving involved in getting him back and forth to Ashley's, one day per weekend was all that he was going to get. I had no choice but to try and minimize the amount of unstructured time that he had in his life, and Ashley's place was clearly the biggest source that I had identified that needed to be addressed. The next thing I did was prohibit him from spending any more time at the skate park for the interim.

I knew that the excessive time he had been spending under the skate park atmosphere coupled with bad decisions had been the source of all this and therefore logically it needed to be off the table at least for the time being in order for him to rise above everything that was going on. My sister Carol was well connected with many different types of people in many different professions, and after talking with some of her friends, she informed me that there was actually a program in place that was aimed at youth currently using drugs or at risk of doing so that I could apply for. They offered many types of resources in the program, everything from physiologists to counselling to rehab, you name it. If it was something that was tried, tested, and yielded results, it was likely something that was available through the program.

After the initial screening, Josh was approved for the program, so I enrolled him and we began our appointments almost immediately. The whole intention behind this was hopefully to prevent him from potentially taking the step to bigger and more destructive substances in his future life. This was another program that required a huge commitment from Marcy and I to undertake as this organization operated out of downtown Edmonton, and everything about the location of that building made it difficult. From high density traffic, to no parking, to needing a half-day off work per appointment—it was a huge commitment to say the least.

As per usual, none of this had any bearing on Ashley whatsoever. She failed to have anything to do with this, just as she had with so many other things in her kids' lives.

As the months went by, the program seemed to do very little to nothing for Josh. Let's face it, these types of programs only work if the person doing the program is engaged in it and wants to achieve success. It won't work on somebody based simply on the fact that their family wants it to. Josh had been attending because I was making him and only because he had no other choice in the matter. It was brought to my attention from a close source to Josh that he had stated he had no intention of quitting smoking weed anyways, and because I could only keep him under my thumb so many hours a day, he still had plenty of opportunities and—from the sound of it—had been taking advantage of them.

After nearly a year of appointments, we pulled the pin on the program as it seemed we had gotten about as far as we were ever going to get with it and investing anymore time and money into it was senseless. Things certainly weren't going terrible with Josh, he was attending school as he should be and not skipping or anything like that, but he was definitely lazy, and the classes he had chosen and the low marks he was achieving in those classes were a clear indication of just that. I encouraged him to get a part-time job, which he did, and this enabled him to make a few dollars for himself and presented an opportunity for him to learn the value of money.

I also hoped this experience might help shed some light on the importance of a good education and how achieving that good education would allow him to do so much more with his life. Between school, work, and his hobbies, he was a busy guy, and that was exactly what he needed.

In terms of hobbies, Josh and Edward had discovered an indoor skate park in Edmonton, and it was a pretty cool place I must say. I would always pay admission for one kid, and in all fairness, I felt Ashley should pay the admission for one kid as well as they both enjoyed the same activities.

By the time you factored in admission, lunch, and snacks you'd be looking at almost thirty dollars per kid for the whole day. The first weekend that Josh and Edward had planned to both attend this indoor skate park together, I told Edward in advance to ask his mom for thirty dollars so he could go. He showed up with nothing as Ashley failed to give him any money claiming to him that she didn't have any.

I have no doubt she didn't have any cash. I mean, how could she? She didn't even have a job. I felt bad for him, and I wanted him to be able to enjoy the day with his brother doing the things that they liked so I texted Ashley and I told her I could give

Edward the thirty dollars he needed for the day, but it would have to come off my support payment to her at the beginning of the next month. She agreed that would be fair and so that's what I did.

As the months went by, especially during that winter when it was thirty below zero Celsius, my kids were really enjoying this indoor skate park and were frequenting it nearly every weekend that they were both at our house. And just like the first time around, Ashley would text me and ask if I could give Edward the money he needed for the day and knock it off my support payment the following month. I wasn't crazy about the arrangement, all it did was ensure Ashley didn't have any responsibility putting any money aside for him for days we had something planned, but I was always just happy that he at least got to go and was able to just have fun being a kid doing something that he enjoyed. I was doing it for Edward not Ashley, but apparently she must have seen things differently.

I remember in the middle of one month receiving a text from her asking me if she could grab two hundred dollars from me from my upcoming support payment the following month. I was shocked she would even ask. I told her no way in hell; the support payment was due on the first of the month and not a day sooner. The straw that really broke the camel's back though came shortly thereafter.

Josh and Edward were wanting to head to the indoor skate park one weekend and that morning Ashley texted me and asked if this time I could give each of the kids thirty dollars for the day deducted from my support payment and then she added in the text and I quote:

"Make sure the kids know where the money is coming from."

I couldn't believe it. Make sure they know where it's coming from? Well that's simple, it was coming from me. No matter how you slice it, that money was coming from me plain and simple. How could she possibly twist it into her mind that she was somehow paying for any of this stuff will always be something that boggles my mind. Nonetheless I was done with it. I told her I wasn't her personal bank machine and there would be no more advances on that support payment going forward.

That also meant, unfortunately, that if she didn't give Edward the money he needed for the skate park or whatever activity that we had planned prior to him coming over, then he wouldn't be able to go, and in fairness to him not being able to go, then Josh wouldn't be able to go either. So really at the end of it all, who did it really affect? The kids of course. As time went by, Josh continued to work his part time job, and I began to encourage him at that point to start prepping himself to take his driver's test so that he could get his license and start driving himself to and from work.

I had been transporting him back and forth up to that point, and typically a couple nights of each week, he would work until eleven and by the time he would get out to my car when he was done cleaning everything up it was eleven thirty. We would get home, and by the time I was crawling into bed, it would be midnight, and I was finding the mornings at work following those late-night pick-ups I was extremely tired. I told him I would pay for his license once he passed the test, and from there, we could look at getting him a vehicle which would not only get him to and from work and school, but also offer him some additional freedom in his life.

Basically, I was working towards trying to help him gain life experience and acquire the things in his life that he was going to need in the future. Ashley on the other hand was doing the exact opposite with Edward and not pushing him to do anything at all that replicated real life experience.

And though I had long realized this about Ashley, and it formed the root of my anxiety when it came to Edward, I had no real appreciation for just how sideways things had drifted. But I was about to find out.

Thirty-seven

I was at work one day and, at about nine in the morning, received a phone call. I didn't recognize the number, and when I answered it was the assistant principal from Edward's school. Her name was Brenda, and she informed me that he had not been attending school and that they had been trying to get hold of Ashley for a few days to discuss it but had been unsuccessful in establishing contact with her.

I assured Brenda that I would establish contact with Ashley, and upon doing so, I would ensure that she in turn called the school. I called Ashley and left her a message informing her that Edward had been missing large blocks of time and that it was something that needed to be addressed. Upon calling me back she claimed she hadn't received any calls as Edward had apparently blocked the school's number on her phone, which was why they were unable to get hold of her.

As per usual, she wouldn't accept responsibility for anything. I'm sure the fact that she couldn't be bothered to give a shit about what was and what wasn't happening in his life had absolutely *nothing* to do with everything that was unfolding at that time. I can promise you it would have taken a hell of a lot more than Josh blocking one phone number on my phone to prevent me from knowing something was going on at school, especially at this magnitude. To this day, I'm positive Ashley knew full well what was happening and simply chose not to acknowledge it.

As it turned out, it wasn't long before I'd be meeting Brenda for the first time. Because Edward was still under the age of sixteen, he was legally required to attend school full time. At that time, the ministry of education had an attendance board in place charged with enforcing the rules and regulations of the education act. If a student was missing an excessive amount of time from school, the attendance board would be notified of the situation and begin their investigation.

From there, arrangements would be made for a meeting between the student, the parents, the attendance board, and the school to discuss why that child hadn't been attending and to put corrective actions in place. If the child was under sixteen years of age, that corrective action would be geared towards the parents who were expected to put measures in place to assure that their child attends school. If the child was over sixteen, the ultimatum may be given to them directly to either attend as they should or risk being withdrawn from the program to prevent the waste of taxpayer dollars and school resources.

I received a call from Brenda, and she notified me that the attendance board had inquired to the school as to when they could arrange for that first meeting, and she presented me with the date that had been set so that I could also attend.

When I did finally meet Brenda for the first time, on the day of the attendance board meeting, I could tell straight away that she was a no bullshit type of person and was convinced—although I have since been reassured by her that this in fact was not the case—she was less than thrilled to meet me.

I could have sworn by the look in her eyes that she thought I was an uninvolved parent who didn't have the best interests of his kid at heart. Having said that, I can also say—in her defence—if my gut feeling about our initial interaction is on some level correct, I don't know what other conclusion she could have possibly drawn, for in all the time Edward had now been attending her school, this was the first time that she had ever laid eyes on me. Couple that with the fact that Ashley had likely been telling her, from day one, that I actually *was* an uninvolved parent, and I wouldn't have blamed her one bit for her view on me at that time.

However, this woman was no fool, and whether she was aware of the circumstances or not, I don't believe that it would've taken her long anyways after our initial meeting to see that things might not be as they appeared to her right out of the gate. I'd like to make mention that, over the course of the next two or three years, I would come to greatly respect this woman on both a professional and personal level. I came to greatly value the advice and opinions that she afforded me at different times along this journey, and I found her input to always be accurate, relevant, and well presented.

What I learned about Edward in our initial sit-down together with the attendance board was really shocking to me. Ashley pled ignorance in all this, claiming that she knew nothing about his absenteeism and pretending as though she was just as shocked as I was to hear what had been going on with Edward. In my opinion, she did a really shitty job of convincing *anybody* that she was genuine in her concern. It was clear that she just didn't care, and I believe that was obvious to all parties involved.

How could she possibly lay around all day long with a schedule devoid of any responsibilities and still not know that Edward wasn't in school? What was she doing all day long? Where was Edward all day then? Ashley's claim of having no clue about any of what had been going on here might have been somewhat believable if she had full-time employment and was busy dealing with the day-to-day goings on of a normal adult, but she wasn't.

She wasn't away from her home ten hours a day at work, affording Edward the opportunity to fly under the radar and do whatever he wanted undetected. She knew full well he wasn't attending school, and I'd bet that he spent a good portion of this missed time from school at home with her. If Edward had still lived at home with us, yes, we undoubtedly would have had our issues with him regarding different things, but him not attending school because he couldn't be bothered to wouldn't have been one of them. Not a chance.

It became quickly evident at this meeting that this lack of attendance was not something that was going to be taken lightly. I'd like to point out that this certainly wasn't something that I took lightly either, but as I was soon to find out, things had escalated to a higher level than I had anticipated. It was made clear in that meeting that, if Edward didn't begin to attend school on a full-time basis, then the attendance board would begin implementing monetary fines and not just on Ashley, on me as well.

After some serious discussion between all parties, the attendance board offered up one last opportunity for Edward to get his act together and get back on track, making it clear that if he didn't, they would bring the hammer down.

I expressed to Edward the importance that he follow through with the commitment that he had made that day and made it abundantly clear that if he didn't there were going to big problems on the horizon starting with me.

Back home, although Josh was attending school every day, he really wasn't doing all that well either. I always attended the parent/teacher interviews for my kids, and every single time I would go to find out what had been happening with Josh, I would always walk away completely blown away and filled with a sense of pride at the end of each interview.

The teachers would all say the same thing about him. They would tell me that he was amazing, very well mannered, that he didn't have to be talked to constantly, and if he did, talking to him once was all it took. He wasn't derogatory or ignorant towards them or any other students, he was just a real genuine nice guy with a sweet personality. Even as we would walk up to the table to sit down to talk to them, you could tell by the look in their eyes that they had a real soft spot for him.

Unfortunately, Josh's sweet nature wasn't the only thing they all agreed on.

When it came to the schoolwork they all had the same complaint. He didn't turn anything in. He wouldn't complete homework, and he wouldn't exchange any of his free time during or after school to seek extra help or extra time to get things done and submitted for marking. Essentially, he was lazy when it came to school. I used to question the fact that he never seemed to have any homework, and he always claimed that there wasn't any.

When mid-terms or final exams approached, he wouldn't even open a book to study, and at times that became a bone of contention between us. All I wanted was for him to do the best he could for himself by getting a good education, which in turn, would someday pave the road to a good job. I was very fortunate in my life in that even with a minimal education—initially lacking even a high school diploma—I was presented with the opportunity to do undertake an apprenticeship program that, ultimately, found me certified in a trade

As grateful as I am for how everything turned out for myself, the trade-off of education versus physically demanding job came at a price to me. I am in my forties today, and I have significant lower back problems from the years of hard work and heavy lifting that accompanied my job, and that now causes me daily discomfort and has significantly impacted my overall quality of life. Even a night of unbroken sleep isn't something I have the luxury of anymore due to the back pain that wakes me up multiple times every night. And it was this sort of grief I want to shield my kids from.

I'm certainly not knocking anyone in the trades. I believe that the people who literally build the world are some of the most skilled and important people on this planet—but the work is hard, and the conditions are extreme at times. I always told my kids to work hard in school so that they could eventually work their way into higher paying jobs where their salary would be based on their wits and knowledge rather than their ability to survive a hard day's physical work.

The issue here wasn't that Josh had a learning disability or even difficulty retaining information for that matter, he just didn't like putting in the effort required to achieve good marks, and he had other things on his agenda that took precedence over the things that really mattered. He actually had a good brain on him and had done nothing more than chosen not to use it. The problem was I couldn't seem to figure out a way to motivate him to want to do better for himself. I was worried that with the ever-changing times and the constant demand in the workplace calling for higher levels of education, the acquisition of a great job might never become a reality for Josh and Edward if they didn't buckle down and start taking their education seriously.

Thirty-eight

As the end of that school year approached, it marked the conclusion of yet another ten months of unnecessary stress generated by both Josh and Edward—and frankly, in my mind, it could not come soon enough. Josh had successfully completed and passed all his classes by a small margin. As for Edward, he'd been attending school since the attendance board meeting months earlier, but it was clear he'd shown up in body only. His mind was elsewhere, and his marks were a clear indication of that.

It was near the end of this school year as well that we first noticed that our dog Jack appeared to be having some issues walking. He seemed to be struggling at times with control of his back legs, and although these changes were subtle at first, it was evident that it was getting worse as time went on. A visit to the vet quickly established that this was likely a neurological issue and not likely something that could be fixed. All we could do at that time was wait it out and see how things were going to unfold for him in the future.

As the battle between Ashley and I continued and her willingness to exploit her children for money remained unchanged, Marcy and I received a letter from the government demonstrating just that. The letter explained that Ashley had been in contact with them and was claiming that she had full custody of not only Edward, but Josh as well—and furthermore always had—and therefore any benefits that the government had paid out for him over the years to Marcy and I had been paid to the wrong people and should have been paid to her.

Obviously, this was nothing more than a bare-faced lie, but that didn't remove the expectation, from the government, that Marcy and I prove Ashley's statement false. The letter informed us that if we couldn't prove that the allegations put forth by Ashley were, in fact, false within thirty days of the date printed on that letter, that they would require full reimbursement of benefits for the six or seven year period in question.

I couldn't believe it when I read that letter for the first time. And to this day, I still can't believe it. She had straight-up lied to the government in an attempt to secure funds for something she wasn't entitled to. This was an all-time low even for Ashley. Out and out fraud. Luckily for Marcy and I, discrediting Ashley's claim was easy to do, but it took time nonetheless to get the paperwork organized and submitted by the deadline. We had to reach out to Josh's school, his dentist, as well as my brother-in-law Henry (doctor) and ask each of them to write a letter stating that they knew unequivocally that Josh had resided with us during the time frame in question.

Josh's school didn't even have a record of Ashley's name on file—during the six or seven years that he had attended their school division since moving in with us, I had never once entered her name into any of his paperwork. On top of that, she had never once attended even a single parent teacher interview and had also never inquired to the school regarding anything as far as his education was concerned. Simply put, the school didn't even know that she existed. Upon receipt of all three letters we packaged everything up and sent it back.

Shortly thereafter, we received a letter back confirming that they had received the envelope and were in acceptance of the documents that we had provided and that the file had been closed. I've often wondered what happened on Ashley's end with all of this when it came to light that she had knowingly lied in an attempt to defraud the government. Were there any repercussions? Or was it simply a letter refusing her request?

With summer holidays upon us again, and the events of the previous summer—Josh smoking marijuana—still very much in the front and centre of my mind, the time had come to put in place some changes to manage the amount of unsupervised time the kids would have during the summer while staying with Ashley. This was my attempt in trying to curb future issues.

Marcy and I knew that, no matter what, the kids were going to be unsupervised whilst under the "care" of Ashley, so we decided that the best way to try and manage that would be to split the parenting time during the summer into eight one-week blocks instead of two one-month blocks. Ashley agreed only because that arrangement worked for her as well, and so that was the blueprint that was then utilized for the parenting time for the remainder of the summers.

To be honest, if Josh and Edward hadn't spent any time with Ashley over their summer holidays each year, it would have been fine by me (and in truth likely better for them). I know that sounds like a selfish thing to say, and I understand the importance of kids spending time with both of their parents, but not when that time holds no value to one parent and becomes nothing more than an unstructured and uncontrolled period as it had every year with Ashley in this case.

Marcy and I always ensured that we had plans, activities, and care in place during our time with the kids in the summer. Those plans typically included a minimum of a couple of days of us all going away together somewhere and just hanging out. Now, I'm not saying that every time we went out on one of these little excursions we always made the greatest memories—but we tried. We were typically strapped for cash, so these undertakings were lean to say the least, but it was the principle of all of us hanging out as a family that really mattered.

I would typically book two and a half weeks off in the summer, and Marcy would do the same, and that ensured that we had the coverage we needed to watch the kids plus a few overlapping days that we could share with each other. On top of that, Carol and Henry would typically send the kids to a summer camp annually at least once—sometimes even twice—for a one-week outing.

Needless to say, Josh and Edward were busy for the four weeks that they would spend with us during the summer holidays, and because they were teenaged boys, that's exactly what they needed. I remember wondering to myself why Ashley couldn't just plan some activities for the kids as well just to keep them busy during the four weeks that they would spent with her over the summer instead of just letting them run wild to dabble in things that they shouldn't have been. But of course, the answer was simple. She just didn't care.

Thirty-nine

It was around this time that Ashley informed me that she had papers to serve me.

Apparently, she felt I was concealing money from her, and so she had gone ahead and acquired one of her legal aid lawyers and had begun the court process yet again. The whole thing was ridiculous to say the least. Here Ashley was, after all these years, still unemployed and still trying to exploit her children in any way possible to supplement her income and nothing more.

And remember, this wasn't about her coming up short on money she needed to properly look after Edward—she barely spent anything on him—this was about nothing more than gaming the system for all she could get. Edward was still dressing in the same rags that he always had since she had taken back custody of him even though there was an ample amount of money being redirected from my paycheque to her every month to properly cover his expenses.

She actually had the gall to suggest I drop by her place on my way home from work so she could serve me. I told her if she wanted to serve me, she could drive over to my house and do it there.

When I did get the papers from her, I opened the envelope from a lawyer by the name of Brian Knight and began to pore over the information inside. There was a request for financial disclosure, and it was a very detailed request. I had to provide all financial documents for the previous twelve months from any and all bank accounts with my name on it as well as any and all credit card statements with my name on it for the previous six months. On top of that, I had to provide my tax assessments for the previous three years and pay stubs for the previous three months.

That was a large portion of information that I had to compile for Brian, and it took me a few hours to get everything together and dropped off at his office. Included in the paperwork I received from Brian was also Ashley's financial information from the previous three years, which was essentially three single documents showing that she had made between six and nine thousand dollars in each of those three years.

Ridiculous.

Josh had a part time job during school, and he was generating over ten thousand a year. I was very uncomfortable providing all my financial documents to Ashley, not because I had anything to hide, but because the documents contained sensitive information including account numbers and balances that I didn't feel that she should be privileged to see.

When the court date arrived, it was just another typical child support hearing like the others I'd attended. Brian had found nothing out of place with my financial history, which I knew would be the case anyways. Still though, I remember the morning of that court date waking up with the familiar sick feeling of anxiety in my stomach, knowing that I had to be at the courthouse in a couple of hours.

I was representing myself, as per usual those days, and that in itself had a tendency to cause me anxiety. Marcy accompanied me again as she had in the past, and her mere presence there afforded me the strength I needed to stand and face the unknown. Of all Ashley's lawyers, this guy was the worst. There was just something about the way he presented himself, something about his approach to things, and something about his face that just drove me nuts.

I couldn't fucking stand him, and I found it hard to not tell him that's how I felt—although I'm sure he couldn't have cared less.

Hell, he may even have felt the same way about me for all I know. Before we were set to go speak to the judge, we met in a small room outside of the actual court room to discuss some details and try to reach an agreement on things prior to entering the court room. During our negotiations, Marcy entered into conversation with Brian regarding the income that Ashley had reported through her tax assessments. She communicated to him it was unrealistic to use those numbers in calculating Ashley's contribution of child support payment for Josh.

A quick calculation of the minimum wage at that time over the course of a year gave us a number hovering around twenty-seven thousand dollars. That was the minimum Ashley could make working a full-time job and, therefore, was the only number that could realistically be considered as her income. Without a doubt, I believe a judge would have agreed with that logic and may have imputed Ashley with that number as a fair income.

After Brian put some thought into it, he came to that same conclusion, and so he agreed he would base her income on that twenty-seven thousand per year. In a twist of fate, with the increase in income imputed to Ashley, her child support payment for Josh increased *significantly,* and as a result, my payment to her actually decreased.

I couldn't believe it. Her plan to try and extract more child support from us had actually backfired on her.

Had she just left well enough alone, she would have been better off. What was strange about the whole court process this time around was how... *detached* it felt. Things between Ashley and I had been over for so many years that all the emotional underbrush had long since burned away. Now all I wanted was to be done with her forever.

Other people in those court rooms were often very much in the heat of the moment of their custody battles trying to hash out all the details. I had been apart from Ashley for well over a decade at this point, and yet here I was time and time again even after all that time had passed standing in front of a judge about the same shit, and I was sick and tired of it.

Under normal circumstances people go to court during the initial stages of their separation or divorce to get the details of everything worked out... and then they get on with their lives. But Ashley had managed to drag it out into this strange awkward dance that made no sense to anyone but her.

As the summer and the latest round of court dealings drew to a close, it also marked the end of any last scrap of normality that remained in Edward's day-to-day life and the beginning of a steady decline into chaos.

Forty

When school started that year, it was evident from his grades the previous year, that Edward was now very much behind and was going to require not only a modified learning program to achieve success but a much different attitude as well. Naturally, the school was fully aware of the struggle Edward was experiencing in his studies and understood where that struggle could potentially lead if some type of modified curriculum wasn't put into place.

So a meeting was called by the assistant principal Brenda to discuss the best course of action to get Edward back on track. She had taken note of how Edward seemed to have interest in technology, so she came up with the idea of him working in the library on the computers to complete some of the courses that he was taking instead of sitting in a classroom full-time doing it. She anticipated the change in scenery from the classroom to the library and vice versa each day might be effective in keeping him interested and on target, and I completely agreed with her vision.

He was also put into contact with the school counsellor, who was also very professional, and she began to work with him as well. Anybody would agree, I'm sure, that this was some amazing initiative on the part of the school. With two thousand other kids under the same roof, it wasn't like the staff on site didn't already have their hands full as it was—this went above and beyond their obligations to Edward.

The sad thing about it, though, was that no amount of support offered by the school could ever make up for the dysfunctional life that Edward was living day in and day out. The utter lack of expectation, accountability, and direction from Ashley in his day-to-day life meant he would never breathe a single breath of success despite all the initiatives that had been put into place to help him accomplish just that.

As the year rolled on, I kept myself in the loop as best I could with the school by seeking updates periodically, but that was the best I could do at that time, considering I worked a full-time job, and Marcy and I were raising three kids under our roof at that same time. Sadly, it became clear within the first couple months of school that, once again, things were not going the direction that we had all hoped that they would even with the changes implemented on Edward's behalf.

As if that wasn't enough going on with him, it was right around this time that a call came in from the school informing me that they had found some drug paraphernalia on him. I think it was a pipe if I remember correctly. I can honestly say, when I heard that, I was completely shocked because I had no idea that he had started using drugs. This was where it became evident that the issues we had been dealing with were bigger and more deeply rooted than we had originally thought—or at least they were going to be in the future.

To this day I don't know exactly when Edward started to use marijuana, but it if I had to speculate I'd guess it had something to do with Josh when he had started dabbling in it. I'm certainly not passing *blame* to Josh with that statement, as I do believe that we are all responsible for our own decisions, actions, and outcomes, but likely that is where this introduction had occurred, and sadly, from there, it would alter the path of Edward's life.

After the school had discovered the drug paraphernalia on him, Brenda was quick in arranging a meeting so that the discussion could take place as to the best approach moving forward. This was serious; we were addressing nothing less than a burgeoning substance abuse problem. At that initial meeting Brenda suggested the school put in a referral to the same organization that I had enrolled Josh in previously when he had started using marijuana.

The benefit of having the school make the referral was that it streamlined things and help move Edward near the front of the line. I was in agreement that this was a good route to go although after the results that I had with Josh when he was in the program, I was a bit skeptical as to what we could expect with Edward who was much more difficult in general.

Previously I had been fully prepared to do whatever was necessary for Josh—for all the good it did—but I wasn't convinced though that Ashley would even make a commitment like that and adhere to it with Edward. I just felt that, as it became more and more inconvenient for her to get him to and from these appointments, she would eventually just stop taking him prior to any results being yielded. Then there was the question of whether the addictions program would even be helpful in steering Edward. As the old saying goes: You can lead a horse to water, but you can't make it drink. That's really what we were looking at.

With Josh, I fulfilled my responsibilities each and every time in assuring he made it to his appointments, but after a while, it was clear that he wasn't engaged in it and so there was no point in continuing. Unfortunately, the scenarios between Josh and Edward were quite different. Josh was still functioning in his life as he should have during those times, and he had been the whole time. That wasn't the case with Edward.

In my mind, he needed this program to work for him or all hope might be lost. Regardless of whatever outcome there had been in the program with Josh, we still needed to try with Edward, and so, on the back end, the school submitted their request to have him enrolled in the program. As I had hoped initially, the process moved swiftly, and the first meeting between everyone was scheduled shortly after that referral.

The initial meeting with the representative from the addictions program was held at the school in one of the boardrooms. Upon sitting down to begin the discussions, the school counsellor who was also in attendance informed us all that she had caught Edward in a small web of lies that morning as to where he was supposed to be in class—and upon calling him out on it, he had told her, straight-up, to fuck off.

I looked over at Ashley in disbelief when I heard that, and she seemed completely unconcerned by it. Apparently, Edward talked around—and even to—Ashley like that often, so I guess that's why it didn't seem like an issue to her. To me though, I clenched my fists in rage when I heard that, and I swear if he had been in that room with us, I would have choked him out. Alright maybe not choked him out, but I definitely would have demanded he apologize to the school councillor for being such a dick even if that would have meant me forcing him to do so.

I wasn't surprised to hear of Edward's dishonesty in the meeting that day. That was another issue that had been ongoing for some time now and had started growing exponentially to the point where he couldn't even keep his stories straight anymore. He was untruthful about everything, and it didn't seem to matter what he was talking about.

During that meeting, we all talked about the different things that we were seeing and hearing, and everyone was given time to provide their input into the situation. As with the last meeting that we had, everything Ashley said undoubtedly carried the scent of bullshit with it, and it appeared as though she was trying to paint a picture of a mother who had been working very hard with her child and had reached her wits end. I took every single thing she said with a grain of salt.

The school kept a detailed log of everything that had happened, and when you read that log, it was clear that Ashley was just as big a part of these problems as Edward was, and she might actually be a hindrance to him in trying to turn things around. Even simple requests from the school to Ashley wouldn't materialize which only reinforced that she wasn't genuinely invested in trying to help turn things around with him.

When he would fail to show up for school, they would try to contact Ashley, and she would excuse all his absences for no good reason. The log the school kept was very accurate, was many pages long, and painted a very vivid picture of exactly what was going on not only in school but what was obviously going in the background as well. I remember during one part of the discussion regarding Edward's use of marijuana, Ashley piped up and stated her concern and then admitted to all of us that she had started to buy him cigarettes in a hope that would curb the marijuana use. She stated that she would rather him smoke cigarettes than marijuana.

I remember thinking: are you serious right now? First of all, purchasing tobacco products with the intent to provide it to a minor is illegal and a crime of it's own. Secondly, two wrongs don't make a right, and providing Edward with tobacco in the hope that it may help to curb his use of marijuana was completely asinine.

At the end of the meeting, a similar treatment plan to the one Josh had undertaken in the addictions program was put in place for Edward. This included an appointment at their office once or twice a month where Edward would have the opportunity to talk to a psychologist, and they could work towards the root of everything that was going on in his life.

Of course, Edward knew that there had been a meeting scheduled that day regarding the behaviour and performance issues he was having, but that knowledge, apparently, didn't faze him at all because nothing changed with him or the decisions he was making making for himself moving forward from that day.

Forty-one

It was shortly thereafter while skipping school one day, Edward got caught shoplifting from a store near the school. Of course, I knew nothing about it until quite some time after it had occurred because Ashley kept stuff like this from me. Needless to say, I was pissed when I heard about it. He was very fortunate that day as the vendor chose not to press charges against him, but the constable that dealt with the situation requested that Edward do some community service at the school.

Instead of genuinely working hard at the community service he had been given in an attempt to prove to everyone that he acknowledged the mistake he had made and was owning up to it through that hard work, he basically blew it off. According to the school, during the time he was supposed to be doing his community service, he spent much of that time on his phone instead of working, and the custodian reported finding the tools and materials he had been given to do the work laying around the schoolyard.

The school also had clear documentation showing that whenever Edward did attend his classes he did little more than sit and stare at the floor or the wall. The computer time that he was given in the library—the opportunity to do some of his courses outside of a classroom—he pissed away playing online games. It was clear he was on a path of self-destruction, and it seemed that there was no changing that.

The addictions program he had enrolled in obviously wasn't doing anything for him either, which didn't surprise me because, to be honest, I don't even know if he was attending it anyways. If Ashley couldn't even get him to go to school, how was she going to get him to go to this program? To this day, I don't fully know what the outcome of that program was for Edward, but I do know he didn't attend it very long or very often before he was done with it. I tried talking to him about what was happening in school and, out of frustration, even went so far as trying to force him to attend and put the required effort in, but it was to no avail.

It was during the school intake this year that Edward turned sixteen, and because of that, the outcome in response to his actions this time around would be much different than the previous year. The school had been very patient in their attempts to lead him to a path of success, but in April of 2017 the inevitable happened, and Ashley made the decision to withdraw him from school.

The ridiculous thing about it though was that neither Ashley nor Edward mentioned anything about it to me whatsoever. They isolated me from the truth as they had always done—almost like they thought it wasn't any of my business. Perhaps they thought that if they didn't tell me maybe I wouldn't find out about it. I knew that things obviously weren't going as well as I had hoped they would in school, but I didn't realize how far gone things were at that point.

I asked Edward every time I saw him how school was going, and his non-committal response was the same every time: "Good." Never once did anything even close to the truth come out of his mouth, and why would it? Ashley had instructed him not to say anything about it. Word of Edward no longer attending had been communicated to me from the school during one of my follow-ups, and I was beside myself when I heard the news. I called Ashley immediately because I wanted to know how the fuck all this shit had gone down without hearing a word about any of it.

I was still the other parent in this equation, and Ashley had an obligation to keep me in the know of anything going on with Edward, be it good, bad, or otherwise, and yet even with something as huge and life altering as this, she still didn't feel she needed to fulfill that obligation. I know you might be thinking to yourself that maybe an update periodically with the school wasn't enough. Maybe I should have done more. Maybe I could have prevented something like this from happening. The bottom line is that there was no way that I could've changed the end result of any of this while Edward was still living under Ashley's roof. I really believe that.

As I have said before, Edward was the product of his environment, and so long as he remained in that environment, nothing was ever going to change. Nothing could ever change. I told Ashley if Edward wasn't going to go to school, then he needed to get a job and start paying for his own expenses. She said she was in agreement with that—but was quick to inform me that regardless of whether he was working and paying bills or not, she still expected a child support payment from me.

Once again, it was crystal clear that her primary focus—and quite possibly her only concern in any of this—was in ensuring that child support payment stayed intact. Her concern for the fact that he was no longer attending school seemed to be non-existent, almost as though she felt it was negligible or something. I remember wondering how she was going to communicate to Edward that he needed to get a job and wasn't allowed to just sit around all day when that is exactly what she did every single day. It was a shining example of the pot calling the kettle black if I've ever seen one.

She didn't have the ability to leverage him to get a job through the threat of kicking him out of the house because she needed him living under her roof in order to collect a child support payment from me every month. To absolutely no surprise, Edward didn't work even one single day during those four months that he was off from school, and as a result, he learned no life lesson whatsoever in the process. I'm not sure exactly what he was doing during that period of time, but it certainly wasn't anything constructive I can tell you that.

I wasn't sure, at that point, if Edward was ever going to get back on track, but to my relief, he did return to school at the beginning of the next year to give it another go. Much like the previous year, this one started off with meetings at the school to voice discussions about the best possible way to help get him on track and generate enough interest in his studies to motivate him to want to achieve success. Unfortunately, by this point, things were becoming much more complicated by the day as more and more obstacles began to come into play.

Because Edward had not completed the majority of his classes from Grade 10 the previous year, there were core classes that needed to be completed and passed before he could make the natural progression to the next level of each, and this of course, was only to going to add to the mountain of work that he already had. If he planned to graduate with the kids that he'd been attending school with the last couple years, it wasn't going to be easy.

I knew that there could be any number of potential outcomes as to how this all played out, and for me, that was very concerning because I had a similar experience myself (though under different circumstances) when I was around his age, and I knew what that end result had been for me.

In my case, I had been kicked out of my house because I wasn't getting along with my parents, and the ongoing challenge of trying to survive on my own assured that school quickly went to the wayside. My attendance at school had become very sporadic, and inevitably I found myself expelled. I made plans to return to school the following year to carry on with my studies, but that proved to be more difficult than I had anticipated, but not for any reason that I had expected.

Upon returning to school, I had many classes that I needed to make up, classes I had either failed or hadn't completed prior to being removed from the program the previous year. On the first day back, as I was going to each different class to meet the teachers, I discovered that in each of these classes the kids I would now be learning with, were all at least a year younger than I was. All my friends that I had been going to school with for years now were taking classes at least one grade higher than me.

I felt awkward around these younger kids because I didn't know any of them, and because of the age gap, I was embarrassed in front of my peers for not being in classes with them where I should have been. It was because of these obstacles that I quickly lost interest in my schooling and my attendance began to diminish because of it. Eventually I knew that there was no way I was going to achieve success with any of it, and so I ended up dropping out as a result.

To my relief, things looked like they might shape up a bit differently for Edward. During the design of her personalized learning plan for him, Brenda had provided a potential solution that I thought was a great idea, one that might help to prevent him from winding up in the same type of situation that I had found myself in years back. She proposed a hybrid type of learning plan where he could attend normal classes with his peers for some of the material and do correspondence for some of the other stuff that he was missing from the previous year. If he could buckle down and work hard in school during the day—and at home on correspondence at night—for the duration of the school intake that year, some quick calculations concluded that it still wasn't too late. In theory, he could still catch up to where he should have been, which would ultimately have found him graduating on schedule and with his classmates.

I held high hopes that Edward would be able to comprehend the importance in all this, make a commitment to it, and then follow it through. But unfortunately, that wasn't in the cards. He carried the same attitude and performance issues from the previous year right into that next year without even missing a beat. And as one would expect, the results of his schooling didn't change either. He was achieving very little to nothing in the classes that he was taking, and his attendance was inconsistent from day to day.

Forty-two

At that point, Ashley was still in a relationship with Mark and had been for a good two years. And although their time together seemed to represent the most stable times Edward had ever seen living with his mother—especially when it came to maintaining one address—things were not as neat and tidy as they appeared from the outside.

I got my first glimpse into what things were like for Edward living under that roof one night as I stopped by his place on my way home. He had left his scooter at our house the last time he was out and had asked if I could drop it off. It was eight thirty on a weeknight, and I was coming off an overtime shift. I jumped out of my truck, grabbed the scooter, and proceeded to walk up the sidewalk to his townhouse.

When I was about twenty feet from the front door, I heard a voice call out to me from behind a bunch of tall trees in the darkness of the back alley. I couldn't make out a face, but I knew the voice to be Edward's.

"Dad, don't go in there. They're fighting."

He was sixteen at this point, and his voice carried a tone of panic, and I was instantly concerned for his safety and well-being for more than one reason. Number one: being a child, regardless of age, and bearing witness to your parent or parents in a heated argument with unknown actions and outcomes is terrifying and could very well lead to long lasting mental effects. Number two: it was late at night, pitch black outside, and in a very questionable part of Edmonton known for the common occurrence of random shit going down, and here he was wandering the streets with nowhere to go after being forced to leave his house until things had calmed down.

I told him to get in the truck and that we were leaving. When we got on the road, I told him that he was going to have to come home with me because I refused to leave him in a position like that. He instantly backtracked on his story and tried to reassure me that everything would be fine and that I could just drop him back off at home. I think he was concerned that if I did take him home with me that night it would impair his ability to smoke marijuana, and that prompted him to try and get me to take him back.

He texted Ashley and told her that I had him in my custody and wasn't planning on bringing him home that night because of my concern for his safety. She told him he was good to come back home at that time and that things had calmed down and been settled—all was well. I called bullshit on it, but Edward was adamant that I take him back, so I did.

When I dropped him off, I reminded him that I was merely a phone call away should he need me, but as he walked away towards his house, I had a uneasy feeling in the pit in my stomach. Was I wrong in letting him go back in there? Had I just endangered him by letting him go back in there? I didn't feel right about it, so I drove a couple blocks up the road, pulled over and searched online for the phone number for child protective services. I found an emergency number and called it. I was on hold for about ten minutes before I finally got to speak with somebody. I told the woman on the phone about what I had stumbled upon that night.

She listened and then suggested that ejecting a child from the home during a time of a major conflict like that was sometimes an effective measure. Yeah, *sometimes,* I guess, but certainly not at nighttime in the middle of a major city. I certainly didn't feel it was a good situation. After talking with her for ten or fifteen minutes, it appeared she didn't feel any wrongdoing had taken place in any of what had happened, and so we ended the phone call.

I threw my arms up in the air in frustration and went home, where an uneasy feeling shadowed me for the next couple days. Was it situations like this that had prompted Edward to want to start using substances such as marijuana in the first place? Was he just looking for an escape from the realities of his life, one that marijuana provided? I learned later that these arguments, many of which were drunken in nature, were something that had occurred frequently under Ashley and Mark's roof, and when I put myself in Edward's shoes, I just couldn't imagine what it must have been like living under those circumstances.

However, that was only one component of the dysfunctional setting that he lived in each day. Ashley and Mark always had roommates living in their home with them as well—a revolving door of different people, most of whom were questionable to say the least. I often wondered what type of influences some of these people might have had on Edward, and that in itself worried me. I remember, one night, Marcy and I stopped by Edward's place to pick him up for the weekend. As per usual I would text him when I would get to his house and let him know to come out. It would typically take him a few minutes to come out, and on this particular evening we ended up waiting about ten minutes for him.

As we were sitting in the car talking, a guy walked past in a black leather jacket then hung a right and headed up the sidewalk towards Ashley's place. Marcy and I took note of him as he walked by and then we watched in horror as he stopped, removed a very large hunting knife from inside his jacket, and proceeded to conceal it by shoving it down the back of his pants. He then walked over to Ashley's front door, opened it, and walked in. He was living there. We seriously could not believe what we had just seen. A minute or two later Edward came out the same damn door and proceeded to jump in the car so that we could go.

Even though he was coming home with us, I had never been quite so worried for Edward's safety as I was at that moment. When I got home, I texted Ashley immediately and told her what Marcy and I had witnessed and how a boundary had now been crossed that significantly compromised the safety of Edward. In my opinion, the possibility of an event of horrific magnitude occurring caused by this person was extremely high. Walking around with concealed weapons was not normal. Ashley made a good show of seeming shocked by the information I had just relayed to her, but to this day, I don't know if any of that reaction was genuine.

She assured me this person would be gone immediately, but do you really think that made me feel any better about any of it? Fuck no. After witnessing what I did that night, I could only imagine the many different scenarios that Edward must have witnessed behind closed doors that he probably shouldn't have.

I told Ashley that I planned to talk with Edward to see if he felt that the possibility of coming back to live with us might be a better arrangement in assuring his safety and success in school. She actually had the gall to tell me that I was only doing it because I didn't want to pay her any more money in child support, and that I didn't have the right to try and persuade Edward to come back—even though that's clearly what she had done.

The truth is me wanting him to come back home with us was way bigger than any child support payment could ever have been in the overall scheme of things. This was about so much more to me. His safety, his emotional well-being, and his future were the only things motivating me to try and get him back home even though I knew the stress that would follow with his return and the impact that it might have on other parts of my life could be devastating.

At one point I even contemplated telling Ashley to let him come back home to us and I would continue to pay her child support regardless, but I knew from a financial perspective that we couldn't afford to do that. Ashley's claims that I just didn't want to pay child support anymore were unfounded, and because I've been on both sides of the fence—as both the primary parent dealing with the day-to-day stuff and also the person making the child support payments—I can assure you if you are doing your parenting job properly, making a child support payment is the easier of the two options.

The truth is I actually took it even one step further because, for four years, not only did I take on the role of primary parent of both Josh and Edward—and all the time and expenses associated with that—but I also did so without any help from her. If I never cared about these kids, I would have taken what I believe to be the easier way out and simply exited their lives years previous and made my child support payments until they grew up.

Ashley claimed to me that Edward was doing the best that he ever had and he was on the up and up, but the fact of the matter was that he had pulled multiple suspensions that year just as he had in previous years since he'd lived with her, and this information had been well documented by the school. It was also clearly documented that, at that point, Edward had been missing about ninety percent of all his daily classes, constantly being caught lying to the administration staff at the school, had someone calling in to the school to excuse his absences by claiming they were me. Hell, he would literally turn and run away from the administration staff when they saw him on school property and attempted to talk with him.

Does it really sound like he was doing better than he ever had? I did eventually have the opportunity to sit down with him and talk about what his plans for the future were and how he felt about possibly moving back home with us, but as with any communication I was having with him those days, the conversation was one-sided and he didn't have much to say. He didn't make it clear as to what he wanted to do, and it was left as an open-ended conversation in which I told him to think about it and get back to me.

He never did.

I think it was pretty obvious to him with the polar opposite rules in place at our house, combined with the immense control over him that living on an acreage offered Marcy and I, it wasn't going to work for him and the things on his agenda. He wasn't searching for a quiet, well structured, safe place where he could concentrate on the things that really mattered like school. He wanted to be somewhere where no one would notice if he was high, or wasn't in school, or wasn't at home, and didn't care anyway even if they did notice.

Marcy and I had so many things that we could offer to him, but *not caring*... that wasn't one of them, that was something that we would never be able to offer him.

In the winter of 2018, things between Ashley and Mark had come to a halt. I don't know why, and to be honest I don't really care. I'm only mentioning this because, when that relationship did inevitably end and Ashley was back on her own, that was when the moving around began again—and just as she had done so many times in the years previous, she took Edward with her wherever she went. After all, he was her child support meal ticket.

On their initial move away from Mark's residence, Ashley and Edward moved in with some people she knew, and they both began sleeping on a couch during that time. Josh was unable to visit them every second weekend during that time, and I can only speculate it was likely due to a lack of space.

Ashley did eventually secure a place to live, but unfortunately the townhouse that she chose to move into was nowhere near Edward's school, and that wasn't something that helped with his already suffering attendance record.

As February rolled around that year, it turned out I was in for a big surprise and not a good one at that.

Forty-three

I was at work one day, at this point I was working as a maintenance plumber for the local government and as I was going about my daily duties, I received a notification on my phone in the form of an email. I opened it up and it was a message from one of the credit bureaus that I had just recently signed up for. This was a free website on which you could sign up and see your credit score and monitor it.

I had been seeing their commercials on TV often, and so one night I decided to sign up, and as it turned out, making the decision to do so actually saved me a great deal of grief. The email I received was a notification of an inquiry that had been made on my credit bureau that day. I was surprised to see that because I knew I hadn't applied for anything credit related for around three years, so I jumped online and signed in to my account—and sure as shit, there it was.

An inquiry had been made that morning by a lending agency for a personal loan that had been applied for online using my name and credentials. This lending agency was well known for their payday loans and their thirty-plus percent repayment interest rates—essentially, they were nothing more than a legalized loan sharking type of organization, and certainly not someone that I would be dealing with for my finances.

I knew right then and there that there was something going on with my credit, and so I began the process of trying to get to the bottom of it all. This would be a much more complicated process than I could ever have imagined. I began by calling the credit bureau that had posted the inquiry, and after waiting on hold for over thirty minutes, someone finally answered and just as quickly the call was dropped. I couldn't believe it.

I called back and began the waiting process again until I finally made contact with someone. Upon answering all the security questions they had in place to protect my identity and verifying to them that I was, in fact, who I was claiming to be, I informed them of the fraudulent activity that I believed had recently taken place on my file.

I was told that, to begin the process of undoing anything that had occurred, there were some forms and other paperwork that I would need to fill out first and send back to them. Upon receipt of the requested information they could then launch an investigation into the fraudulent activity in my file. Right after I got off the phone with the credit bureau, I called the phone number of the vendor attached to the credit inquiry on my file from that morning.

After navigating the vendors corporate directory, I was transferred to their fraud department where I talked to a woman who was very helpful in assisting me. She informed me straight-up that the corporation had established this was likely a fraudulent transaction almost from the beginning, and therefore, no money ever did transfer hands.

Naturally, I still had a million questions about it, and I wanted to try and establish who this person was and where they had gotten my information from to begin with. I was concerned because I shop frequently online from many different vendors, and if my personal information had been harvested from one of those sites somehow, I wanted to know so I could follow it up with those vendors as well. The woman from the fraud department opened up the online application that had been submitted to them for the loan initially and proceeded to tell me that there was actually a bank account number and a name that had been provided to them as a place to deposit the funds from the loan upon its approval. I asked her what the name on the account was and when Ashley's name rolled off the end of her tongue, I was in complete disbelief.

Though perhaps I shouldn't have been.

Ashley had taken personal financial information gleaned from our last court appearance and had attempted to defraud me by applying for a loan using my name, income, and credentials. The woman from the fraud department recommended I file a police report immediately and provided me with all the corresponding information regarding the loan such as date and time as well as her direct contact information.

She told me if I wanted to include her contact information in my report to the police that they could also contact her in confirming the details of what had happened with all this. I took a couple hours off work that afternoon and went down to the nearest police station to file the report. This was a bit of a process, and as one might expect due to the busy atmosphere of a police station, there was some waiting involved in having my turn to talk with an officer.

When we did finish filling out the police report, I was told that, within a day or so, I would receive a call from another officer and he would come meet me to discuss things in detail and make a plan as to where it would be taken from there. One might ask themselves as to why somebody committing fraud would ever put their actual name to something like this, and in this case it was because of the policies the vendor had in place to prevent this exact scenario from happening. Without providing a legitimate bank account number with a legitimate name and address attached to it for deposit of funds from the loan—should it be approved—they wouldn't have done it. Ashley knew that there was no other possibility of accessing these funds if they were released, so she provided her banking information to them for the deposit.

The following morning, I received a call from the police officer who was going to be investigating my case, so I called my boss booked an hour off work, and the officer and I met shortly thereafter. I told him everything that I knew regarding the situation and explained to him how my sensitive information had come into possession of Ashley. I then reminded him that the way Ashley's name had come into any of this was through information provided to me by the vendor—in other words, I wasn't simply acting on a hunch.

He told me that, at the beginning of the following week, he planned to show up unannounced at Ashley's place and confiscate all her electronic devices and have them searched by a tech at the police station for the information the vendor had provided to them. He then instructed me not to reveal any information about it to her so that she didn't have the opportunity to delete any evidence of what she had done from her devices prior to them being taken away.

The next thing I did was to begin the process of trying to undo everything that had been reported to the credit bureaus. Due to the urgent nature of the situation at hand, and in the best interests of protecting myself, I had to get done it immediately. I ended up taking more time off work in order to get that information into the proper hands at the credit bureaus, which I knew, in turn, would help to expedite the process of getting things back under control. This wasn't just a simple matter of filling out a couple of forms online and emailing them back to these people. This required printing multiple documents that had to be completed by hand, dated, signed, and then faxed in alongside photocopies of my passport, my driver's license, and a pay stub to verify to them I was in fact who I was claiming to be.

I had to complete this entire process for both credit bureaus, and because I didn't own a fax machine, I ended up having to go to an office supply store and pay them per sheet to fax this information to each of the credit bureaus. After I had completed faxing all of the documents to the necessary recipients, I was instructed, during my final conversations with the bureaus, that there were still a couple more steps that needed to be taken by me in order to further protect myself.

The first was to put a fraud alert warning on both my credit bureaus, which would require any vendors to physically contact me by phone and verify my identity through personal questions prior to granting any credit in my name. This was a free service and, once active on my file, would remain there for a period of six years. Secondly, I needed to register what had happened with the anti-fraud agency of Canada. This is a government run organization that collects information and criminal intelligence on different types of fraud.

By the time I was done all the phone calls, meeting with the police, data entry, time spent online, and all the necessary faxing, I had used eight hours of vacation at work and had spent nearly fifty dollars in the process, and for what? I should make mention that all this occurred just nine days after I had given Ashley her child support payment.

I never did hear anything back from the police about it ever again, and so I don't know what the outcome or fallout was for Ashley. Hopefully she felt some repercussions, but if so, I never heard about them. Nonetheless, I had put all the necessary precautions in place to protect my identity moving forward, and if nothing else, it was an eye-opening experience for me regarding identity theft and how to protect myself from it in the future.

Forty-four

In March of 2018, Edward's school decided again that he should be withdrawn from the program. Enough was enough, and rightfully so. He was still missing the majority of his classes and absolutely nothing had changed. According to school documentation, Ashley was in agreement with the decision and claimed that she didn't have the ability get him to attend or even care about school for that matter, and so essentially, she was admitting that she had long since given up on him.

Perhaps if she had taken his last withdrawal from school the previous year as an opportunity to lay down some real world groundwork by encouraging him get a job and pay bills instead of allowing him to lay around high for months on end, the motivation he needed to be successful in school might have already been in place.

I couldn't blame the school for their decision. They had gone above and beyond what anyone could have ever expected of them. As in the past, word of Edward no longer attending school didn't come from either him or Ashley—as it should have—instead it came from the school itself during another one of my follow-ups to see how things were going and how he was doing. When I learned of Edward's withdrawal from school this time around, it seemed to carry a feeling of impending doom with it. I wanted to be positive and hold high hopes for him, but deep down, I knew that it was too far gone now, and that wore heavily on me.

On a more positive note, March of 2018 also marked Josh reaching the ripe old age of eighteen. It was hard to believe, and I was excited for him as he was near the completion of high school and had been making plans to attend post-secondary schooling. Marcy and I decided to have a little get together at a popular pizza place to celebrate his birthday, and we invited a bunch of family to celebrate with us including Carol and my parents.

We scheduled dinner for after work that day, and the plan was that I would pick Edward up from Ashley's in my travels so he could join us as well and then I'd run him home after we were all done. When I picked him up that day, it was within a week or so of the school pulling the pin, and so in truth, I was pissed off about it, and when he got in the car I starting giving him the gears (though I wish now that I hadn't).

I wasn't doing it because I wanted to be ignorant to him, I was doing it because as a stakeholder in his future, I wanted to know what the fuck his plans were. I wanted some answers, and as per usual, he didn't have any to offer me. In his mind, his future was at the bottom of a pop can, and considering the circumstances he had now put himself into yet again, that wasn't acceptable by me. When I asked him if he planned to get a job, he said he didn't know and truthfully that terrified me.

The last thing I wanted him to do was follow his mother's example. Ashely had, for his entire life now, done nothing at all but lay around day in and day out. I told him that his mother's lack of employment and lack of contributions to society were unacceptable and that he wasn't allowed to follow that path in his life. I told him to look at the big picture and tell me, since he had moved back with Ashley, whether things in his life had gotten better or worse.

Then I asked him if he felt he could live with that type of lifestyle for the rest of his life because, without the proper direction and decisions, there would be no choice in the matter. As per usual, he didn't have anything to say, and he just sat there staring down at the floor blankly. When we arrived at the restaurant, everyone was there, and we sat down and I began to look over the menu for what I wanted to eat.

I noticed that Edward hadn't even opened his menu, so I called over to him and asked what he was having. He said he wasn't having anything, and he just sat there staring down at his phone typing into its keyboard. I felt bad that I may have upset him the way I did, but he needed a reality check in the worst possible way—and clearly Ashley wasn't ever going to give him one.

I honestly hadn't *planned* on lecturing him that day or getting into with him; we were all meeting simply to celebrate Josh becoming an adult and nothing more, but anytime it's come to my children and their futures, I've always worn my heart on my sleeve.

Shortly after I ordered my food, I saw Ashley's car pull violently into the parking lot followed by her jumping out of her car and barreling into the restaurant. Apparently, Edward had been texting her regarding me giving him the gears and voicing my concerns about his future, and he had communicated to her that I was talking shit about her even though it was nothing more than the truth.

Once she was inside, she scanned the restaurant floor, saw where I was sitting and then proceeded to approach my table and threaten me.

"You better get the fuck outside right now," she said. "Before I cause a shitstorm in front of your little family."

When she said that to me, my daughter Anna (3) and my son Michael (8) were within earshot and very much aware that something bad was unfolding. They had never met Ashley, and so as far as they were concerned this was just some deranged stranger who had approached me. That was my immediate concern in all of this—I didn't want my young kids to witness something that might cause them stress or anxiety in the future, and so with a smile of reassurance to them and as cool as a cucumber, I excused myself from the table and told them I'd be right back.

I locked eyes with Marcy as I stood up, and I could see that she was pissed that Ashley had decided to make an appearance the way she had that day—I could tell that she was at the end of her rope with it. I was quick to take things outside and out of view of my kids, and it's a good thing I did because things escalated quickly.

Outside, she got right in my face and told me that I had no right to talk about her and that I was a piece of shit. Well for the record, if there was *anybody* on this fucking planet that I had the right to talk shit about it was her. This is a person who had used me for years for anything she could possibly get her hands on through lying, cheating, or any other means necessary, had put my children in the middle of any and all of the bad situations she had put herself in, and had even gone as far as stealing my identity not even a month prior to this altercation, and now she was standing there telling me that I was a piece of shit?

The things that I had said to Edward about her that day weren't even spoken in an attempt to diminish her in front of him anyway. I was simply trying to drive home the point that what passed as normal for Ashley was anything but. That was the message I was trying to send. That's it. Make him realize that real life wasn't sleeping in every day and staying high around the clock instead of going to school or getting a job.

As Ashley was going off on me, I heard my mom's voice behind me, and when I turned around, I realized that she had followed me outside when I had exited the building—and just like that, the arguing between Ashley and her began. I do appreciate my mom and the things that she has offered up to me over the years in the form of different types of support and help, but this wasn't one of those times. This was my battle, and my mom really had no place in it. I told her she needed to go back inside, and I would deal with it.

She was hesitant but she did go back inside if somewhat reluctantly. Both Ashley and Edward were very disrespectful towards my mom that day, and although I wasn't surprised at Ashley's demeanor towards my mom, it bothered me deeply that Edward chose to take that avenue with her as well. He had no reason to show his grandmother any disrespect.

At that point, all I wanted Ashley to do was leave the restaurant and crawl back under whatever rock she had come out of before she had decided to taint Josh's birthday celebration with her presence. The truth is I didn't even have the time of day for her anymore, and so in an attempt to diffuse the situation instead of blowing it wide open—as I certainly could have—I calmly told her to go home and we'd have to discuss it later.

She was still trying to get me fired up at that point, but I just couldn't be bothered to care. Honestly, she just wasn't worth it. She told me that I would never see Edward again and they both walked away, jumped in her car and drove off. I went back into the restaurant, sat down, and pretended like nothing even happened in an attempt to reinforce to my little ones that everything was alright.

The really unfortunate thing that did come out of all the events that occurred that afternoon was the embarrassment Josh was forced to endure because of it. When I looked into his eyes and saw him smile to me upon my return to our table after the incident, I could tell that he was embarrassed about how this had all gone down, and I felt really bad for him. I still have that image of his face in my mind, and it still bothers me. He didn't deserve that, especially not on his birthday. This is another shining example of the mentality of Ashley though. Any normal functioning parent would simply have either picked up the phone or set up a meeting with the other parent to have a a conversation about it heated or otherwise and would never have had the desire to show up at their kid's birthday celebration to try and aggressively settle it then and there.

I'm not sure what Ashley's objective was that day, but other than confirming to me that she was an even bigger idiot than I thought, she didn't prove a damn thing—who knows maybe she didn't even have an agenda maybe it was nothing more than sheer lack of discretion and impulse control.

I don't know what communication was exchanged between Edward and Ashley prior to her arrival at the restaurant and whether or not what I had said was blown out of proportion or taken out of context, but regardless he shouldn't have been texting her about my concerns anyway. I'll admit that I was disappointed in Edward over the events that transpired that day, for I felt that he too was partially responsible through his actions for what occurred. I'm certainly not saying that I was innocent in all this and that everything that transpired was brought on by Edward. I realize that the simple act of talking to him the way I did that day, essentially set that ball rolling.

I can actually remember thinking to myself prior to everything unfolding, as I was talking to him, that perhaps I should just keep my mouth shut about things and not let my emotions and worries about his future run wild and get the better of me. The problem is that I have always struggled with great difficulty keeping silent when I've been forced to watch my children fail—especially when Ashley is at the root of it.

It had never been more obvious that day that I needed to take a break away from Edward. I didn't want to, but for my sanity, I had to. I talked to Marcy about everything that evening, and she agreed time away was the best thing I could do at that point.

Forty-five

It was right around this time back at home that the inevitable finally arrived for our family. It was only ever a matter of time really. Our dog Jack who was now at the ripe young age of 5 had met his match with the ongoing health issue that he had.

His walking had deteriorated by this time to a point that he was barely mobile anymore, and as much as I didn't want to do it, my sister reminded me that the only humane thing to do was to put him down. I knew she was right, and so I went ahead and booked the appointment as much as I dreaded doing so.

A couple days later, I took a half day off work so I could come home and spend time with Jack. I really hated knowing the end was so near for him, and although I tried to stay strong for him, I could tell that he could sense my despair. The whole experience still haunts me to this day. Very few times in my life have I ever felt as down as I did the day that I left the vet's office without him. This also marked the first time in many years that I cried. It makes me emotional just thinking about it.

RIP my Jackie Boy.

Following that, as the months came and went, I was ecstatic to watch Josh graduate from high school. That was a big deal for me because, of course, it wasn't something that I'd managed to achieve myself and so I was super proud of him for getting as far as he did. Even though I knew that he didn't have a stellar diploma to propel him into any university course his heart desired, at least he had a diploma, and we could work on acquiring the courses he would need for his post-secondary in the upcoming year.

Carol and Henry were amazing in their endless support to my kids in furthering their education and had offered them an amazing opportunity should they choose to take it when the time came. They were willing to cover all tuition and book costs related to whatever post-secondary training the kids may want to pursue whether that was in university, college, or whatever.

I can't begin to express enough how much pressure that took off Marcy and me from a monetary standpoint because, in truth, we couldn't afford to pay for a long-term post-secondary degree as much as we wished we could have. On top of that, if the kids were to maintain passing marks and the right priorities throughout the process, Carol and Henry were also willing to pay for all living expenses during their schooling. They even went as far as to offer the choice of where they wanted to stay during that time be it at a dorm at the school, in an apartment nearby or in their basement if they wanted.

They also put forth that they would provide a daily spending allowance so that only school would have to be a priority and they wouldn't have to work a part-time job during those years of schooling. Nothing less can be said about that offer other than amazing. Over the course of the previous year, Carol and I had been prompting Josh to spend some time doing a career investigation and start trying to narrow down what he might want to do for a living once he completed school. He was definitely struggling in trying to nail down what he wanted to do, and I had to be reminded on more than one occasion from Carol and Henry that it was a harder thing to do than what I was thinking in my mind.

I guess after nearly twenty years of breaking my back under the worst conditions imaginable and then seeing all the amazing jobs that there were in the world, I expected it would be easy for him to make a decision based on something that interested him. Keep in mind, I left myself no options way back when, and took the only opportunity I ever had and, therefore, had never experienced what he may have been going through in all this.

In my mind, when it came to Josh's future, the sky was the limit. Carol and I took him to some open houses at different universities and colleges around Edmonton to feel things out, and I thought all the different amenities and programs offered at these places were amazing. Every place we went was super cool, and in my mind, I was sad that I never had the chance to experience it myself, but I was really pumped that Josh would.

As the summer holidays arrived that year, plans were underway for him to start his post-secondary in the fall, and he had narrowed it down that he would study to acquire a bachelor of arts degree with the possibility of maybe teaching someday. Due to not having the necessary courses from high school required for the program right out of the gate, he would have to upgrade at the university his first year. Upon successful completion of that upgrading, he would then be cleared to proceed into the avenue that he had chosen.

Carol and Henry went ahead and enrolled him at the university for upgrading and everything was set to go. When September rolled around that year, Josh moved away from home and into Carol and Henry's place so as to attend university. It was the very day he left that it sunk in just how many years had gone by and how I could never have those years back again.

At home the two extra rooms downstairs that Marcy and I had worked so hard to build now both sat empty. To this day, I have left Josh's room the way it was the day that he left.

Edward also made a return to school that year, and once again, I was relieved that he had done so. Even though I knew that the odds of him achieving success were stacked against him because he was so far behind—but the fact that he made a return yet again introduced the possibly that he might succeed.

We hadn't seen each other much up to that point, and once Josh had moved away to Edmonton the frequency I would see either of them would diminish even further. Weekends typically meant that both Josh and Edward would stay at Ashley's house (where they could do the things they wanted to that they couldn't do at our house).

When I found out Ashley was fully aware—and even approving—of some of the activities under her roof I was appalled. The bottom line was as simple as it was depressing: Because of the restrictions we had implemented under our roof, the simple act of coming home for a weekend wasn't something either one of my kids had an interest in doing, and so I never saw them very much from that point forward. I guess I know in my mind that, someday, they'll come back to me, and until then I just need to be patient and keep in touch with them the best I can.

I got myself back in the loop with Edward's school so I could keep tabs on what was happening with him, and right from the get-go things were not looking good. The more things changed with him it seemed, the more they stayed the same. Just like the previous two years, he was still missing the overwhelming majority of his classes.

When Ashley and Mark had split up in the months previous and she had relocated to a new place, instead of being a block and a half from the school, Edward was now thirty or forty blocks from the school, and when I confronted him on why he hadn't been attending he claimed he had no way to get there and that Ashley wouldn't drive him because she didn't have any gas.

I remember thinking, *what the fuck?* Because communication between Ashley and I had long been severed now, I told him to tell her to buy him a bus pass as I had literally just made a child support payment a couple days prior to cover those exact type of expenses. Ashley claimed she didn't have any money to buy him a bus pass, and so with no choice in the matter, I took it upon myself to get him one so that he could at least get to school every day.

I went to the nearest convenience store and inquired about a bus pass. They informed me it was about a hundred dollars for a monthly pass, but if my kid was in school, that I should buy one through the school and it would be at a subsidized price. When I called the school to purchase his bus pass for him, it came to eighteen dollars.

That's right. Edward claimed he had been unable to get to school because Ashley had neglected to buy him an eighteen-dollar bus pass.

Unfortunately, even after acquiring the bus pass for him, it was brought to my attention—during one of my ongoing follow up calls with the school—that his attendance hadn't improved whatsoever. I guess he must have been using the bus pass I had bought him to go and do whatever it was that he was up to during the day.

At the end of the October 2018, Edward was removed from the school program once again due to lack of attendance. He didn't even make it two months that year. As always, that was a real stiff dose of reality for me, and the worry I had been living with for the last two years about what his future held returned full force. This time, however, I chose not to lecture or preach to him about it because there was simply no point or merit in doing so.

I had another sit down with Brenda at Edward's school shortly after his dismissal to discuss everything, and as per usual, she gave me some very insightful advice. She explained that even though Edward had chosen a path that was the complete opposite of what I ever wanted for him, the groundwork that I had instilled in him over the course of his life, through my actions, would someday come full circle. Things like always being around for him no matter how far Ashley had moved away and always providing him with a safe, secure, and quiet home. Also things like teaching him that a family sits down together for supper with the TV off and talks about their day; or physically showing him that I cared enough to never give up on him and take the easy way out during the epic battles that we had.

She explained it using the analogy of a brick foundation where everybody who had been involved in Edward's life had put some bricks into that foundation including herself. She explained that the bricks I had put in were very much still intact and integral as to who Edward was as a human being, and although these bricks were perhaps deeply buried at this time, they would eventually come back to the surface someday. When they did, they would help to guide him in the right direction, which in turn, would hopefully lead him to live and love a normal, happy, and successful life until such time that old age took him back to the weeds.

She then went on to explain that the only thing I could do moving forward was to reinforce to him the fact that I loved him and that I was there should he need anything. She explained how that could be something as simple as a text message periodically or a phone call telling him that he was in my thoughts. She used the analogy here of these messages being like little seeds planted in his mind. Seeds that, in time, would grow and evolve into something much bigger, seeds that would always let him know that I loved him, I was there for him, and that I wanted nothing but the best for him.

As per usual, the only concern Ashley had with any of what had gone down revolved solely around that child support payment. She made it clear, yet again, that she expected it to be paid to her regardless of whether Edward was attending school or not. I briefly entertained the idea of maybe going to court just to see what a judge would say about it, but because Edward was still under the age of eighteen at that time, I'm sure if it had gone to court that I would have been ordered to pay anyways, so I saved myself the hassle and just continued to pay.

Forty-six

During this time, Josh was busy with his upgrading at the university he was attending, but the truth of the matter was he wasn't fully immersed or invested in what he was doing.

It didn't take long before it was clear that, even though he had made the right decisions for himself in terms of the steps he had taken up to that point, it wasn't going to last, and he was about to let it all go to the wayside. There were signs leading up to what did eventually happen, and those included the amount of time he had been spending at Ashley's place.

At first it was just on the weekends, but as time went on, he began going there one night a week and then two, and so on and so forth.

In December of that year, when Josh announced to Carol and Henry he was not intending to return to university in January for his second semester, it really came as no surprise. I was terribly disappointed in his decision to discontinue his education, but as Henry pointed out to both Carol and me, it was Josh's choice to make.

Initially, upon making his decision, Josh had planned to get a job and save up some money to secure an apartment for himself and Edward. From what I understand though, Ashley was quick in communicating to him that Edward would not be allowed to move away from her until he had two thousand dollars saved up, which obviously wasn't something that was even possible considering the fact Edward didn't even have a job and never had up to that point. This was nothing more than Ashley's way of maintaining control of Edward and assuring the child support payment she relied on so heavily continued to be paid to her.

Even more disappointing was when Josh announced, shortly thereafter, that his plans had changed, and he was going to move in with Ashley and Edward instead.

When I heard that I knew that his future was now completely up in the air. I remember during the previous year, when Josh was struggling with choosing the career path, he had made mention to me at one point he may just want to enter the work force instead of attending university and he might do so by starting in a trade. Although I wasn't thrilled to hear that, one can certainly hash out a good living though a trade, so it wasn't something I was completely against him pursuing.

At the time, I offered him a deal. I told him if he decided he wanted to enter the work force instead of attending post-secondary—be it through the trades or whatever—that he could continue to live at home completely free of any expenses for another two or three years so long as he saved most of what he was making so he could put it towards a down payment on a house when the right time came. I knew that I would never have the financial capability to cut a cheque to any of my kids for a down payment on their first houses to get them started, and so this was the best thing that I could offer to them.

It was almost hard to believe that, after everything everyone had offered and done for him, that it was Ashely he would choose to move in with. I had to really stand back and look at it from the outside before it made sense as to why it went the way that it did. Even though there were many of us that were willing to offer support to Josh in any way that we could, none of us were willing to help support him in the lifestyle that he wanted for himself.

Except for Ashley that is.

She had no issue in helping to support it whatsoever. One thing that became evident was that there would be no way of helping him out once he had moved in with Ashley without also helping her in the process. Giving him money to pay rent or buy food was the same as giving her money to pay rent or buy food, and I refused to do that. She was still utilizing Edward anyway she could, and because he was still under the age of eighteen, she was collecting over eight hundred dollars a month in child support from me—money which she was primarily using for herself—and so helping her any further was out of the question.

Carol talked to Josh in January of 2019, just few days prior to him moving out in the hope of convincing him to consider moving instead into a small quiet one bedroom apartment by himself where the bills were manageable instead of moving in with Ashley, but that wasn't something that appealed to him. She picked up a vibe off him almost as though he was troubled by the thought of living by himself. Perhaps that's why he chose the path that he did in all this.

Undoubtedly the desire Josh had to live the lifestyle that he longed for seemed to remove all logic from his mind, and I'm not sure the reality of what he was actually doing to himself and his future ever came into play. I understand that he was young and probably didn't have the ability to foresee the outcome of his actions, but he had a lot of awareness brought around him on where the decisions he was making would potentially lead him in the future, and that still didn't seem to have any type of impact on him.

In their never-ending support of my children, Carol and Henry made mention that the offer to pay for schooling—should the kids decide in the future to take it seriously and make a solid commitment to the work involved in acquiring a ticket, diploma, or degree from a post-secondary organization—would be something they were willing to revisit should that time arrive.

Josh's search for work was successful, and it wasn't long before he found himself employed. I'm proud to say that, to the best of my knowledge, he is at least a tax-paying contributing member of society—but sadly the work that he does is very laborious and due to the fact that it isn't one of the core trades that require four or five years of apprenticeship training to acquire a ticket in, the pay is on the lower end of the scale. With little to no room for growth or movement from the positions that he works in, his future is limited in what he is currently doing.

Essentially, one could say that things are at a standstill in his life, and to be honest, that is frustrating because he could be doing so much more. They both could be. It was during this time, as Josh made the transition into once again residing with Ashley, that a disconnect between my two eldest boys and me came into play.

A disconnect that is still very much present today.

Forty-seven

Everything I have written about thus far has been based solely on fact. I have only written about what I witnessed and experienced first-hand and what is known to me to be fact. However, at this point in the story a level of secrecy came into play—implemented by Ashley and abetted by my kids—which effectively insulated me from whatever was happening with them.

Josh and Edward were both still teenagers, and neither wanted me to know the details of their lives under Ashley's roof nor any of the questionable things that may have been happening there. It was at this point that nearly any details I got about what was happening with them were being provided to me by reliable sources who were connected to them during that time period.

The information was relayed to me to assist in my ongoing efforts at trying to remain involved in their lives and the things that were happening within their lives. I wanted to know what they may be going through or experiencing and not just the things that they wanted me to hear. I wanted an accurate snapshot of what was happening so that I knew how to offer support to them if they needed it.

Although some speculation is certainly present in some of the details I am about to touch on surrounding their day-to-day lives, I can assure you that the statements are accurate as to what did occur.

One of the first things I remember hearing just prior to Josh moving in with Ashley was that when he did move in—at least initially anyways—he'd be sleeping on a couch somewhere. Apparently, with all the subletting Ashley had been doing to pay the rent, she had rented out all the bedrooms including the one for Edward. As a result, *he'd* been sleeping on a couch somewhere down in the basement for an undisclosed amount of time.

I remember the frustration I felt paying eight hundred dollars a month in child support for Edward and knowing that, after doing so month after month, he didn't have a bedroom or even a bed for that matter and was instead sleeping on a couch. Nonetheless, the absence of those things didn't seem to be of concern to Josh whatsoever, and he moved in anyways. The quality of life Ashley provided under her roof was the other thing that had me questioning either of my kids desire to want to live with her.

One night, not too long ago, I received a text message from Edward asking if I could buy some food for him because there was none in the house and he was starving. When I received that text, it was a week after I had made my child support payment to Ashley, and I just didn't have the means to give anymore without it affecting my ability to provide for my own household. It was a terribly upsetting and unsettling text to receive, and I felt horrible about not being able to help, but in truth, I had already done my part for that month, and I had to remind myself of that.

Initially I almost felt like maybe I had been sending a mixed signal in my communications to my kids, as I had always told them if they needed anything to just call me, but this type of scenario wasn't what I meant when I told them that. I meant if they needed a place to stay, some advice, a ride somewhere, an ear, or whatever that they could always depend on me to come through for them. I made mention to him that because he had chosen to no longer attend school that he really should be working a full-time job anyways and been buying his own food.

I explained to him—as I had with other things over the years—that I had *just* made my child support payment to his mother *literally* days before and that it was her responsibility to utilize my monetary contributions for him to assure that he had what he needed. He responded saying she had told him that she had no money, and that there was literally no food in his house. Carol ended up picking him up from home that evening and taking him to go get some groceries. She had no problem whatsoever helping Josh and Edward out in any way she could with whatever they needed, but just like me she had no interest in helping Ashley out through her acts of generosity, which was a direct side effect of helping the kids.

Carol told me that, when she and Edward arrived back at Ashley's place from grocery shopping, she walked a couple of the bags of food they had purchased up to the door to set them inside and the entire house was in a haze of smoke and smelled strongly of marijuana. This was another clear indication of the type of activity deemed acceptable by Ashley under her roof and also provided a possible explanation as to why they didn't have any money for food. I wasn't surprised to hear any of it. It only fortified what I already knew.

Another shining example that really sticks out in my mind regarding the quality of life that my kids were leading occurred when we all got together for brunch one afternoon. When we arrived at the restaurant, I noticed almost immediately that Edward had a very strong odour attached to him. It was a mix of mildew such as what you might encounter in an old basement that is leaking slightly and cat urine.

Having to sit there over lunch with the realization that this is what had become of my son was very difficult for me.

I'm not sure if this was just a one-off thing—perhaps he was just so down on himself on that particular day or week and didn't care about his appearance or personal hygiene—but that was a stiff dose of reality for me and a really hard day. The fact that Ashley wasn't pushing him to look after his personal hygiene be it at home or going out somewhere only backed up the fact that she either just plain old somehow hadn't noticed, or just simply didn't care enough to do something about it if she had.

Marcy and I have always supported an open-door policy at our home with our kids, and I have reiterated that to Josh and Edward time and again that should they need or feel the desire to move back home that the door is always open. I mentioned that to Edward, that day before I said goodbye, that I felt him coming home might be something that was necessary for him to do. He acknowledged that he knew the open-door policy was in place but never once, to this day, have either one of them ever taken advantage of it.

It was around this time the decision was made between Ashley, Josh, and Edward to start looking for a new place to live. Instead of searching for a three-bedroom apartment or something along those lines, perhaps even a place in which some of the utilities might be included to help minimize running costs, they opted to start the search for a house instead.

Between the three of them, there were two who didn't work, and Josh who was going to have to try and figure out how to make ends meet every month when they did make that move. It was during this time of them searching for a new place to live that I became aware that Ashley was still up to no good in the way she was doing business in her personal life. I guess some things just never change. Of course the way she chose to run her life had nothing to do with me, and in truth, I couldn't have cared less about how she did things but the fact that she was passing all her shitty personality traits off to my kids in the process was pissing me off.

Josh had informed Carol that they had found a new place they planned to rent and were scheduled to move in a couple days later. Except a quick glance at the calendar suggested that a couple of days would be around the twenty first of the month. I remember thinking at the time, *who the hell takes possession of a rental property on the twenty-first of the month?* Possession dates, when I used to rent, were always the first of the month or the fifteenth, and so it seemed obvious there may be more to this story than what was being disclosed.

Nonetheless, through whatever means, they managed to scrape together enough money to make the damage deposit on the new place, which they went ahead and submitted to the new landlord to hold the property for them. My belief is that Ashley had made a plan to vacate the townhouse they had been living at the same day they took possession of this new place without providing the required notice—thus leaving the landlord holding the bag with any unpaid rent, any damage to the unit, and cleaning the place up and getting it ready to rent again. I mean that had to be the plan, why else would they be moving into a new place two thirds of the way through the month?

As it turned out, the move didn't go the way it had had been planned, and when the day did arrive, they loaded up all their shit, drove it all over to the new place, and upon arriving made the discovery that the home was legitimately owned and occupied by someone else. Apparently, the whole thing had been some type of scam in the local classifieds, and they had fallen for it, likely under the direction of Ashley, and given away all their money in the process to the scammer behind it.

After realizing they had been duped, they drove right back to the place they had planned to abandon and moved all their stuff back in, which is where they continued to stay for the time being. Josh made mention to Carol about the events that had happened regarding the scam and how Ashley had gone to the police to file a report on what had happened to try and get their money back.

How ironic that Ashley was actually upset that someone had ripped her off when she herself at one point had been dabbling in the same type of activities, illegally trying to part people with their money. Perhaps she was only upset because she had fallen for it and been taken advantage of while she hadn't gotten so lucky when she was trying to defraud me in the previous year.

I'm pretty sure it's just called karma actually.

I don't know the details of how that scam went down, but stupidity had to have come into play. Why would anybody in their right mind give money to somebody they don't know without first confirming, unequivocally, that the person was in genuine receipt of the goods and or services they are securing with those funds. The money Ashley lost in this I chalked up to a *stupid fee*, but I genuinely felt bad for Josh because I knew the money he'd put in for the deposit, he worked hard for, and now that it was gone, it had left him in a bad position financially.

Josh did end up approaching Carol and asking if she could help him out financially due to the hardship, but as per my request, she turned him down. I felt that there was value in this experience, and if Carol had bailed him out there would be no lesson taken from it. Within a couple months of them getting scammed, they ended up legitimately securing and relocating to a house that they still currently rent.

Which brings my story up to present day.

With Edward turning eighteen in November of 2019, I am preparing myself to close a very stressful and long drawn-out chapter in my life so that I can start a new one. One where, at long last, I will finally get the monkey off my back and I can proceed in living my life the way I want to without the dark cloud that is Ashley hovering over me everywhere I go. A chapter in which I can embrace my beautiful wife and glance towards better days after all the hardship that we have faced together over the years. I can't stress enough that, without Marcy, I'm not sure how I would have fared on this journey, but I can certainly speculate and tell you that the outcome likely wouldn't have been good.

I have always drawn my strength from her, and she has always kept me strong. Right from the start of our relationship, this was indeed a complex situation for a young woman to insert herself into, and I've always known that I was very fortunate she actually chose to start a life with me when she could simply have walked away after deeming the situation as being too complicated.

Her choice to become involved with me saw her become not only a staple in my life but also a staple in Josh and Edward's lives as well. I know for a fact that she holds a very special place in the hearts of those two boys and that the bond that she has created with them as the mother that was always present in their lives—even when Ashley wasn't—will continue to resonate within them for the rest of their lives. For me, it literally feels like this whole process has taken an eternity to run its course, and now that the end is near, I'm finding it to be bittersweet.

Obviously, things like not having to deal with Ashley's bullshit anymore and her inability to use the kids against me for her own personal gain are a couple shining examples of the positive changes that are on the horizon. However, the end has also brought light to the fact that these once little kids have since grown up and that, all the days in between, days that have lead up to them becoming adults, are now gone forever.

Due to Ashley and the constant drama and dysfunction she was dragging Josh and Edward though and her endless ploys at trying to exploit them for more money, my mind was never focused on the things that really mattered which were in fact these irreplaceable moments in time with my kids. Moments which added up to days, then months, and then years. I was overwhelmed by the never-ending battle with her, and the only thing I wanted to do was get to the end of it all so that I didn't have to deal with her anymore.

As a dad who is now having a completely different experience raising his second set of kids, it's been really hard for me to accept what I missed out on by choosing the course of action that I did with Josh and Edward at that time. Essentially, I've wished my life away, and I worry now that as an old man I'll die regretfully because of it. I've often wondered if there was another way that I could have dealt with all this, one that would have allowed me to enjoy the time that I had with Josh and Edward, ultimately leading me to a more positive experience and outcome, but because of the other person in this equation and the way things were handled, I've come to the conclusion that the answer to that question is no.

I'm not sure there is any other way I could have come out of this, feeling anything other than bitter and exhausted.

On a more positive note, I do look forward to the near future when I will no longer have any affiliation to Ashley and because I have fulfilled my responsibilities to the children I share with her from both a monetary standpoint as well as a parental standpoint I can relegate her entirely to the past where she belongs and begin concentrating on a future where she is nothing more than a memory.

I do plan to try and support Josh and Edward in their future endeavours as much as I can. And should the time come with their jobs that they are tired of hitting brick walls at every turn due to a lack of education or whatever the case may be, I will certainly reach out to the connections I have made in the world over the years to help get them started into something that will someday hopefully allow them to realize some of their dreams as well.

Just like from day one, when this all began so many years ago, when they were just little toddlers, I still have no intention of ever exiting their lives. The fact that they're both grown men now doesn't change a thing in terms of the commitment that I have for them or how far I'll go for them if need be. Even after everything I was forced to endure, when I look back now, they were worth it, and I would do it again if I had to.

All I ever wanted to do was maintain my involvement with them—instead of walking away and missing out on watching them grow up. I am proud and thankful to say that I was brave enough to take the high road regardless of how difficult that became along the way.

As for the life that Marcy and I have created for ourselves, I have every intention of embracing each moment I can, not only with Marcy but also with Michael and Anna who have given me a second chance to be a dad all over again. They've been instrumental in making me understand how magical these years truly are and have helped me to become a better father to Josh and Edward along the way as well.

Essentially, I plan to put all that has happened behind me and move forward in my life both mentally and spiritually sound toward the amazing things that await me in the future. Someday when the end does arrive for me, whether that's many years from now or only a few, if all my kids are healthy and alive, and I'm still married to my beautiful wife, then I can't ask for anything more, and for that I'll always be thankful.

The End.

Afterword

When I first started this memoir, I thought I'd write something that might offer support and advice to people going through similar circumstances. While I obviously don't wish those sorts of circumstances on anyone, I do hope that, for those who are struggling, this work has been valuable in some way.

Now that I have reached the end of the project, I realize that the advice within might be distilled here for clarity's sake.

1. Never go into court looking for moral validation or recognition; that's not what courts are for.
2. Understand that pursuing legal action for emotional reasons will likely cost you time, effort, and money—and will rarely pay off emotionally.
3. If you've been told how some regulation works, even if it feels ridiculous or inequitable, don't choose to ignore it simply because you feel that you're in the right or that it *ought* to work some other way.
4. Recognize that in any relationship (especially one involving kids) the person who cares less about the relationship has an advantage over the person who cares more. Which is not to suggest that you should care less, only to be aware of the disadvantage you face caring more.

5. Just because something seems inequitable to you, doesn't mean that the system is broken or doesn't make any sense. The system is a blanket that has to stretch to cover hundreds of thousands of vastly different scenarios, and so there will be the occasional foot that is left out in the cold.
6. You are an individual, when it comes to the law, you are not being targeted or punished or victimized regardless of whether it seems that way.
7. Do not fixate on what happens to the other person because that's pointless and will drive you mad.
8. When all else fails, remember the Serenity Prayer:

God, grant me the serenity to accept the things I cannot change,
the courage to change the things I can,
and the wisdom to know the difference.

About the Author

Dunstan D. Arlington is just a typical nine-to-five working-class member of society. With an infatuation for music, writing a memoir certainly wasn't a venture that he ever thought he would embark upon. But no one knows what the future will hold. After a long drawn-out battle with his ex, one that lasted more than a decade and left two kids stuck in the middle, he felt there was possible merit in sharing his experience in the hopes of helping other individuals caught in similar circumstances.

CPSIA information can be obtained
at www.ICGtesting.com
Printed in the USA
LVHW092314060320
649304LV00007B/17

9 780228 820895